D0281456

Solving people-problems

Solving people-problems

Peter Honey

McGRAW-HILL BOOK COMPANY

London · New York · St Louis · San Francisco · Auckland · Bogotá
Caracas · Hamburg · Lisbon · Madrid · Mexico · Milan · Montreal
New Delhi · Panama · Paris · San Juan · São Paulo · Singapore
Sydney · Tokyo · Toronto

Published by
McGRAW-HILL Book Company Europe
Shoppenhangers Road, Maidenhead, Berkshire SL6 2QL, England
Telephone 0628 23432
Fax 0628 770224

British Library Cataloguing in Publication Data

Honey, Peter
    Solving people-problems
    1. Personnel management
    I. Title
    658.3   HF5549   80–41032
ISBN 0–07–084544–1 Cased
ISBN 0–07–084949–8 Pbk.

456   AR   932

Printed and bound in Great Britain by
Antony Rowe Ltd, Chippenham, Wiltshire

Contents

Introduction

If you are a practising manager you will find this book invaluable. It does not matter about your seniority level, the sort of activity you manage or whether you work in a large or small organization. All that matters is that you deal with people.

Even if you are not a manager of people in the literal sense but have a job where influencing people is important, then you will still find this book useful.

Whether you manage or influence people, or both, you are bound to have your fair share of people-problems. If you find this hard to admit, consider how often other people disappoint you by not doing what you want them to do. Run down the accompanying checklist to identify your people-problems and who causes them.

People-problems	*Caused by*			
	Bosses	Subs	Colleagues	Others
Producing insufficient work				
Failing to work to deadlines				
Producing shoddy/slapdash work				
Bad timekeeping				
Being unreliable				
Being resistant to change				
Being negative				
Being awkward				
Getting people's backs up				
Being too autocratic				
Procrastinating				
Covering up mistakes				
Not cooperating				
Being too competitive				
Being aggressive/vindictive				
Being event-driven				
Not developing/growing people				
Not delegating				
Not communicating				
Being overdemanding				
Being too reticent				
Not being assertive enough				
Paying too much attention to detail				
Being flippant				
Being too cold and distant				
Others (please specify)				

This book is about how to solve people-problems like these. It will introduce you to a problem-solving approach that is refreshingly straightforward and pragmatic. The approach focuses on the circumstances surrounding people's actions rather than on people's personality make-up. It therefore does not get bogged down in a morass of underlying complications such as people's motives, attitudes and feelings.

In addition to concentrating on the tangible, observable aspects of people-problems, the approach does not expect you to do things over and above your normal duties, nor does it demand time you have not got. The approach is based on a few sensible principles and is free of gimmicks and jargon.

In 10 short chapters this book shows you how to solve people-problems. It includes numerous examples of people-problems, all drawn from real life, and even concludes by showing you how to solve problems with yourself!

I should like to acknowledge a number of people who have contributed directly and indirectly to this book. Firstly, thanks to the hundreds of managers who have reacted so favourably when I have introduced them to the problem-solving approach described in this book; their enthusiasm first gave me the idea of writing a book about it to reach a wider audience. Secondly, thanks to my colleagues Alan Mumford and Margaret Neal for reading and commenting on all chapters in draft before I finalized them; their suggestions improved the book very significantly.

Finally, thanks to my wife, Carol, and my children, Tim and Katie, for letting me monopolize the study for hours on end and for putting up with so many other inconveniences while I worked on this book.

Peter Honey
April 1980

1. *What are people-problems?*

A problem, *any* problem, is the difference between what you have got and what you want. Whenever you think this difference comes about because of someone's actions or behaviour, you have what we are going to call a people-problem.

It does not matter whether you are right or wrong in your thinking; all that matters is that *you* are aware of a gap between what you have got now and what you want and *believe* it is being caused by someone's actions. The actions may be those of your spouse, your children, your friends, your colleagues, your subordinates, your boss, your competitors—anyone, in fact, and even, as we shall see, yourself.

So, whenever you experience any of the following, you have got at least one people-problem on your hands:
- You believe that someone you are associated with could do better than they are doing.
- You feel disappointed about someone's actions.
- You grumble about someone behind their back.

You complain to someone about some aspect of their behaviour.
Since these things are common, everyday occurrences, it is very likely indeed that you, along with everybody else, have your fair share of people-problems.

If you cavesdrop on any pub conversation, there is a 70 per cent probability (I have tested it) that it will be about people and their inadequacies. Monitor your own conversations and discover how often they are expressions of various disappointments you have with people. Take any daily newspaper and count up how many articles or features are about people's behaviour and the problems it caused for someone else; you will find such articles in the majority. The fact is that people-problems are rife. They are not necessarily dramatic or bizarre, quite the reverse in fact; more frequently they are the day-in, day-out niggles and frustrations we experience with the people we come into contact with.

People-problems, like people themselves, come in all sorts of shapes and sizes: some are trivial, minor irritations, while others are more substantial and seriously impair relationships or performance of a job to be done; some are temporary, others seem more consistent and permanent; some are surprising and unexpected, others are understandable and predictable.

How often do you encounter people who are negative, awkward, hesitant or uncooperative? Do you know people who are too verbose, will not come to the point, will not volunteer anything, resist change, are too autocratic, too soft, disorganized, too aggressive or are too slapdash? And what about the people you know who are argumentative, too compliant, rock the boat,

1

too flippant or are not creative? All these, and many more like them, are people-problems.

Let us look at some specific examples. In this chapter I will describe six different people-problems; in subsequent chapters we shall return to these problems and solve them. The first problem is a domestic one, the others all occurred in a work setting.

PROBLEM 1   THE HUSBAND WITH A NAGGING WIFE

A husband, married for 15 years, very much disliked his wife's habit of nagging him when things about the house were in need of repair. The things were always relatively trivial, like a dripping kitchen tap needing a new washer, the spare bedroom curtain pelmet needing to be secured to the wall, the sitting-room door needing some wood shaved off the bottom to clear a new carpet, and so on. None of the things was exactly urgent and none of them offered much challenge or was likely to push back the frontiers of the husband's do-it-yourself skills—they were all routine maintenance chores. So the husband postponed the jobs and his wife nagged and nagged until they got done.

PROBLEM 2   THE PERSONNEL MANAGER AND THE SHOP STEWARD

At a factory in the Midlands a personnel manager has a considerable problem with a particular shop steward. Hardly a day goes by without the shop steward bursting into the personnel manager's office with some unreasonable demand. Often the demands are absurd and have no chance of being met, but the shop steward still persists in pushing the case in an aggressive manner. Over the years, the relationship between management and this particular shop steward has steadily worsened; there is a catalogue of incidents, including stoppages and strikes, attributable to his activities.

PROBLEM 3   RON AND HIS CIRCUMVENTING BOSS

A middle manager, Ron, has a problem with his boss. After working for him for 18 months, Ron has come to the conclusion that his boss is deliberately circumventing him. For example, his boss frequently talks to his staff (Ron has eight subordinates) about pay and prospects without consulting him. He also allocates tasks to Ron's staff direct without going through him or informing him about it. He also goes to meetings with users (Ron works for an in-company 'service' activity) without taking him along and commits him, in his absence, to providing services. Even when they attend meetings together, Ron often finds that his boss says things at the meetings that he does not agree with, and these contributions are sprung on him without any prior discussion or consultation.

We shall return to these problems in Chapter 3 and show how the new approach tackles them successfully.

The next three people-problems are described in more detail so that we can use them as working examples of how to employ the new approach. In Chapter 3 you will be encouraged to try your hand at solving them using the new approach, and in Chapter 4 I shall give you some solutions to compare with yours.

PROBLEM 4   IAN, THE MANAGING DIRECTOR

Ian is about 40, and for the last year has been managing director of a manufacturing company that operates autonomously but belongs to a big group. He has got very firm ideas on how best to manage people—in general terms he believes that people respond best when the pressure is on. Ian has tremendous energy; he gets into work at 07.00 hours most mornings and stays late each evening. He works extremely hard and expects others to do the same. He is a stickler for detail and frequently sends his managers scurrying back from meetings to collect more facts. Face-to-face meetings with him are more like inquisitions; he adopts a very aggressive questioning style and 'bawls people out' when he uncovers mistakes. He prides himself on his ability to move heaven and earth to 'fix' problems, and his grasp of both technical and financial problems is very impressive. This means that he interferes a great deal; as soon as he suspects a deficiency, he 'pounces' and sorts it out himself.

When there is a problem to be solved, Ian is very fond of gathering all the involved parties together in one room, irrespective of rank or reporting relationships, and forcing the facts out on to the table. In order to bring the truth out (he calls it 'flushing' the truth out), he adopts a very challenging style ('I don't believe you'; 'You are lying'; 'How come he has just accused you of . . .?'; 'You are trying to pull the wool over my eyes'). All these remarks are dished out in public, often to senior managers in the presence of their subordinates. What is more, Ian will keep the group at it all night if necessary, overriding any other commitments. Eventually he succeeds in solving the problem and in getting advance warning about other problems in the pipeline.

Rick, the personnel director, is one of the managers who reports to Ian and particularly resents this treatment. Not only does he find it degrading for a man in his position, he also feels that, as personnel director, it is his responsibility to do something to change Ian's style. Rick is seriously concerned about the effects of Ian's behaviour; he notices that his colleagues are showing signs of stress, they are putting in enormously long hours (trying to keep up with Ian) and they are becoming more competitive towards one another and less cooperative. This preoccupation with Ian has reached absurd proportions—they spend unproductive time talking about Ian in his absence and trying to anticipate his 'next move'. Another alarming effect of Ian's behaviour is that senior directors spend inordinate

3

amounts of time getting the details right so that Ian's probing will not catch them out. Directors who were previously willing to delegate are now less inclined to do so because they feel the only way they can really know what is going on is to involve themselves. The attention to detail means that directors spend all their time on day-to-day issues and are not inclined to do any forward planning. Furthermore, Rick notices that the directors are less willing to admit mistakes than previously; they increasingly try to contain problems and conceal them from Ian to escape his wrath.

Ironically, Ian has complained to Rick that too many directors are 'fire-fighting instead of doing what they are paid to do, which is think'. He told Rick that he could not understand why people thought he was such a hard man: 'Don't they understand that conflict management is all about stimulating alternative courses of action? When I bawl at them, what I really want is for them to go away, think again, then come back and tell me about it.'

Rick decides to set about modifying Ian's behaviour.

PROBLEM 5   OVERLOADED TED

Ted is a specialist marketing adviser in a big organization that manu-factures and sells its own products. He works as a one-man band advising different sales forces on such things as market trends, how to interpret statistical surveys, how to push certain products, and so on. This job takes him out and about the organization a great deal, always in an advisory capacity.

Ted reports directly to the sales director of the organization, a man of similar age and experience (early 50s with nearly 30 years' experience in industry). They get on OK except that Ted very much resents his boss's habit of loading far too much work on him with deadlines that are absurdly tight. This seems to happen whenever Ted goes to him with a work prob-lem. For example, Ted often consults him on the interpretation of statisti-cal data which have a bearing on market trends. Typically, Ted requests the meeting, provides him in advance with the data in question, and goes into the meeting with a series of questions that he wants to find answers for.

Each time, his boss seems reluctant to take any initiative in throwing light on the meaning of the data. Ted has noticed that he often turns questions back by saying, 'That's your province Ted. What do *you* think it means?' Time after time, therefore, Ted finishes up providing his own answers and not succeeding in picking the sales director's brains sufficiently.

This is disappointing enough for Ted but there is worse to come! In-variably, at the end of these meetings the sales director will say, 'Now, have you got a minute Ted? I've just got a few things for you.' This heralds a vast list of projects, queries and jobs to be done which the sales director gives to Ted irrespective of his current work load. Ted, of course, protests and explains why he cannot possibly get through the extra work load by the time the sales director is requesting it, all to no avail. The sales director just smiles and says, 'We're all busy, Ted. See what you can do. I leave it with you.'

So Ted moves heaven and earth to get through it all in addition to his 'normal' on-going work; he works late in the evenings, takes work home at weekends, and so on. After a while Ted begins to wonder whether he is wise in being so compliant. What, he wonders, would happen if he refused to take on the work or did not do it? Ted has always been a conscientious man, however, and possibilities like these go very much against the grain.

PROBLEM 6   BERT, THE SUPERVISOR

Bert is a young supervisor who looks after a small section who process cash vouchers and receipts. He has six girls working for him and one of them, Maureen, is a problem—she does not get through her work quota. Just lately she has been away sick and Bert was interested to find that her stand-in completed the equivalent work quota easily.

Maureen's job involves coding and categorizing incoming petty cash vouchers and receipts. There are two different sorts of vouchers: some need processing on a weekly basis, others on a 24-hour basis. The weekly batch come into Bert's section on Tuesdays at lunchtime; there are usually 600 vouchers in this batch and they have to be processed by the following Tuesday. The daily vouchers vary in number between 20 and 60 per day; they arrive on Maureen's desk by coffee time each morning and have to go to the computer department by 10.00 hours the next day.

Bert is convinced that Maureen is capable of doing the work on time and that her training has been adequate. He is not sure why she takes too long over the coding and categorizing—she does not waste time in any obvious way. She does not, for example, chatter to friends too much or wander around other parts of the building. Bert has approached her in the past and tried to establish why she has not completed the work; she always has excuses or just shrugs her shoulders and looks blank. Bert has even suggested that she looks for another job.

Virtually every morning at present there is a mad scramble to get the invoices ready for dispatch by 10.00 hours. Everyone pitches in and lends a hand, including Bert himself. The vouchers and invoices are always ready by the deadline—it is just that Maureen never gets through the work without eleventh-hour assistance.

What is your reaction to these problems? If you feel they are rather unreal, it is probably because I have not yet described a problem you can relate to

5

closely enough. In fact, the six people-problems cited so far all actually happened; this applies to all the problems used as illustrations throughout this book. There is not a single problem that has been invented. Only names and some minor details have been changed to conceal identities of people and organizations.

Alternatively, you may find the problems unreal because of a sort of 'double standard' that you may be using when reacting to case-study descriptions. For many people the double standard works like this: in real life we may frequently experience people-problems, and even fail to handle them satisfactorily; however, we may react to descriptions of *other people's* problems by claiming that they have been inept in handling them and that we would never have got into that sort of mess ourselves. For example, you can probably see that the husband with the nagging wife has only got himself to blame. Over a 15-year period he has habitually postponed tackling routine maintenance jobs about the house and in effect 'forced' his wife to nag him. Similarly, you may claim that the personnel manager and the factory management have been weak in dealing with the stroppy shop steward; they should never have let him get away with it in the first place. The problem should never have been allowed to escalate. But the fact is, foolish though it may seem, that the husband *did* repeatedly provoke his wife into nagging him, and the personnel manager *was* lumbered with an overdemanding shop steward. Neither knew what to do to get to grips with the problem. Of course, there was a time when they could have solved these problems relatively easily. The *first time* the wife had nagged, for example, or the *first time* the shop steward had been overdemanding, were obviously ideal times to nip this sort of unwanted behaviour in the bud, but, as so often happens, the opportunity was missed. The first time, or even the second and third time the behaviour occurred it probably did not seem very significant. In retrospect, however, it was the thin end of the wedge and it is only when you are well on the way to the thick end that the problem becomes recognizable as such.

This is typical of people-problems—the substantial ones almost slip into being. They develop over a period of weeks, months or even years. Initially the problem does not seem worth bothering about and, before we know it, it has settled down into a predictable pattern that looks obstinately permanent.

So be careful not to 'condemn' the people with the problems I have described in this chapter as incompetent. Ron should not have allowed his boss to circumvent him; he should have sorted it out when the tendency first began to show itself. Rick should have grasped the nettle earlier and done something about Ian's aggressive style. Ted should never have pulled out all the stops and tackled the extra work that his sales director loaded onto him. Bert should obviously have not allowed Maureen to work slowly and consistently fail to process her invoices on time.

In truth, none of these people was, or is, in the least incompetent; they are busy and trying to do their best, and, inevitably, encounter all sorts of problems—not just people ones. The striking thing about all these people is not their incompetence so much as the fact that they recognized they had people-problems and were open enough to admit to them—no mean achievement, as we shall see.

So, in summary, the people-problems we shall be concerned with in this book are all thick-end-of-the-wedge problems—problems that have not responded to a straightforward tête-à-tête, problems that have not been solved by normal, everyday processes. Typically, they have developed over a period of time until they have settled down into a stubborn, persistent and predictable pattern. The problems are entrenched.

A useful thing to do before going any farther is to reflect on a couple of your own current people-problems. Produce a description, just a paragraph or two long, that pin-points the problem as you see it. Concentrate on identifying problems that meet the following criteria:

1. From your point of view, the problem should result from someone else's actions or behaviour (for convenience I will refer to this person as Fred).
2. The problem you have with Fred should be significant to you. It should, for example, inconvenience you in some way rather that being merely a minor irritation (Fred may pick his nose in meetings but this might not actually inconvenience you)
3. Fred should be a person with whom you have regular, frequent contact. If you only encounter Fred once a year, for example, then that is not frequent enough for our purposes; it is better to select a problem with a Fred whom you encounter a number of times in a typical working week or fortnight.
4. Finally, is the problem with Fred a persistent one? Is it a problem with his actions or behaviour that repeats itself time and time again? If it is just a one-off, do not bother with it. It is much better to select a problem at the thick end of the wedge, and preferably one that persists despite the fact that you have had words with Fred about it.

Those four criteria should stand you in good stead in selecting appropriate sorts of people-problems, problems that are both entrenched and inconvenient. Do not try to solve the problems at this stage, just concentrate on identifying and describing them. Solutions come later.

2. *Traditional ways of tackling people-problems*

In Chapter 3 we will be examining a new approach to analysing and solving persistent people-problems, but first we will look at the usual ways people-problems are tackled. This will help you to contrast traditional approaches with the new approach and to weigh up the relative advantages and disadvantages of each.

Let us start by reviewing the options frequently adopted by managers when they are faced with the sort of problems we met in the last chapter.

DISCOUNTING THE PROBLEM

The first approach does not really amount to an approach at all, since it involves ignoring the problem in various ways rather than trying to tackle it. The problem of, say, a persistently poor performer can be discounted in at least four different ways:

1. The manager may deny the existence of the problem and behave as if it did not exist: 'Problems? I don't have any problems. My subordinates have all the problems!'
2. He may admit the problem but belittle its importance: 'I agree the fellow's performance isn't satisfactory but I've more important priorities just now.'
3. He may admit the problem exists but claim that there is not a feasible solution: 'The unions would be down on me like a ton of bricks if I did that', 'There's nothing for it but to live with the problem', 'It's just human nature.'
4. He may discount the problem by again admitting it exists but doubting his own ability to tackle it: 'I've tried everything I know and it still hasn't done the trick', 'There's nothing I can do about it. Others may succeed, and good luck to them, but I'm out of my depth with this one.'

THE PEP TALK

A very common approach to people-problems is to give the offender a pep talk. This can take many forms but it usually involves telling the poor performer that his current performance is not satisfactory and that 'He'd better pull his socks up or else!' Sometimes this approach does the trick, particularly if the 'or else' is a threat that the poor performer believes the manager will carry out if the current performance continues. It also needs to be something that the poor performer actually wants to avoid. Pep talks tend to solve the problem if the poor performer holds the manager in high esteem and if the pep talk happens early on in the history of poor performance. It is not nearly so effective, it seems, if it is saved up over perhaps a few weeks or months of persistent poor performance.

However, the pep talk has a very poor track record in solving many of the more persistent people-problems. Often the improvements are short lived and there is a rapid decline back to the old way of carrying on; this is because the pep talk leaves all the onus for change on the poor performer himself. He might just pull it off if he *wants* to improve sufficiently and has the self-control to maintain the changes in performance without any help from the manager. The pep talk is understandably attractive to the manager since he has so little to do and, if it fails to work, makes it easy for the manager to justify more drastic action: 'I did my best to warn you', 'I gave you good advice but you didn't act on it.' (In other words, 'It's your fault, not mine. I'm in the clear.')

COACHING, COUNSELLING AND APPRAISING

Popular with trainers and consultants, but not nearly so popular with practising managers, is the suggestion that poor performance can be remedied by a coaching and/or appraising approach. In many organizations an enormous investment in time and money has been made in a bid to cajole managers into doing more of this. The basic philosophy is undoubtedly sound: a manager is responsible for the development of his own subordinates; he is the person to set and agree objectives, monitor on-the-job performance and give regular feedback. It can work well providing:

1. The manager has adequate interpersonal skills to handle the face-to-face coaching, counselling and appraising sessions. In my experience, most do not. Striking the fine balance between judging and helping, criticizing and praising, telling and asking is more than most can accomplish. The result is often embarrassing, even bruising, to both parties.
2. The problem is analysed properly. Later in this chapter I hope to show how people-problems are often described in such vague terms that a start cannot be made on their resolution. Analysing problems is more than half way to solving them and yet this is often skimped in appraisal sessions.
3. The session results in a feasible action plan which is subsequently implemented.

Unfortunately, these are rather a lot of provisos for coaching, counselling and appraisal sessions to surmount. This means it is rare for such sessions to bring about lasting performance improvements.

SENDING POOR PERFORMERS AWAY FOR TRAINING

A very popular approach among managers with poor performers is to dispatch them to an off-the-job course of instruction. This has tremendous appeal because the manager is able to comfort himself that he took some action without actually doing any of the dirty work himself. In a sense, he imagines he has delegated his problems with poor performers to the instructors or trainers. This is a temporary illusion, as he usually discovers when trainees return. Off-the-job training *can* work, especially if the poor performance stems from some skill or capability shortfall; it rarely works, however, if the problem stems from a lack of inclination. This is because, contrary to popular belief, a lack of inclination is usually encouraged by the working environment itself, and sending poor performers on a course aimed at changing them without commensurate attention to their working environment is a naïve shot in the dark. The reason why so many courses appear to produce disappointing results is often because the return to an unchanged working situation quickly neutralizes and negates anything that may have been learned on, perhaps, an excellently designed training course.

PUNISHING POOR PERFORMERS
An approach managers brag about but rarely employ is that of finding some way to punish poor performers. The punishments can take many forms: giving them more to do, giving them the most monotonous tasks, holding back an incremental raise, telling them off, breathing down their necks, nagging them and generally making life unpleasant.

Punishment of poor performers is rarely adequate in bringing about lasting performance improvement. Although to the punisher it often appears to work admirably, studies have shown that punishment leads only to temporary suppression of unwanted behaviour and has all sorts of undesirable side-effects. Instead of getting on with the job in hand, the punished people can spend too much time looking over their shoulders seeking to anticipate and avoid punishment. It can also lead to resentment that expresses itself in pilfering, sabotage and activities generally aimed at 'getting their own back'.

GETTING RID OF POOR PERFORMERS
Despite legislation about dismissal practices, there are still plenty of ways of getting rid of people that, if necessary, avoid formal dismissal procedures. A phoney way of getting rid of poor performers is to make them (not their jobs but *them*, note) redundant, often at considerable expense to the organization. Other ways of getting rid of people without appearing to do so are to arrange a sideways move, give them a special project (which is not at all special really), get them promoted, or to ignore them until they leave of their own volition.

Getting rid of poor performers is a way of *avoiding* the problem of how to manage them in a way that gets adequate task performance. Often these ploys merely serve to shunt poor performers around so that their continued poor performance is even more aggravating to a greater number of people.

So it seems that traditional approaches to tackling people-problems often fail

10

to resolve anything; as a result, people-problems abound in most organizations. Often this is rationalized with a shrug of the shoulders by claiming, 'Well, all organizations have their share of dead wood, don't they?' and 'We all have our problems.'

This state of affairs is regrettable but entirely understandable. Managers are usually busy people caught up in an event-driven environment, juggling with a variety of simultaneous, conflicting pressures. People-problems are just one of the many things competing for attention. This pressure, plus the fact that there is widespread uncertainty about how to proceed with people-problems, makes various forms of procrastination inevitable.

Before we move on to look at a new approach to solving people-problems, I want to highlight two snags with the way we tend to approach people-problems. Both the snags seriously impair the analysis of people-problems and, if the analysis is impaired, then so are the solutions.

SNAG 1 THE TENDENCY TOWARDS 'LOFTY' DESCRIPTIONS OF
PEOPLE-PROBLEMS

This is the tendency to describe performance shortfalls in very general, lofty and unspecific terms. In everyday parlance, we tend to use one-word descriptions to sum up a behavioural tendency that we have observed in someone. We talk of people being aggressive, lazy, negative, and so on. Such words are useful as shorthand descriptions but, when it comes to analysing people-problems, they lead to two difficulties.

The first difficulty is that, even though such words are used initially to sum up a conclusion we have reached based upon observations of someone's behaviour, they soon lapse into descriptions of more general attributes. If you describe someone as lazy, for example, strictly speaking you are using the word to sum up a behavioural tendency you have observed in that person. That is fine except that, in no time at all, it is assumed that the person possesses a personality trait of laziness; apart from being nonsense (no one is lazy in *all* situations), it is completely unnecessary to postulate the existence of some underlying trait.

It is more comforting to the manager faced with the problems of a lazy employee, of course, to attribute the cause to a trait of laziness. It conveniently absolves him of any further responsibility; it is the employee's fault. He has this personality weakness and that is that. The manager need look no farther for the causes of the lazy behaviour.

The second difficulty with general rather than specific ways of describing behaviour is that words like aggressive, lazy and negative are too sloppy to aid us in pin-pointing the problem precisely enough. When we say someone is lazy, what precisely do we mean? Is it that they come to work late, take extended breaks and leave early? Is it that they chatter with friends about last night's exploits rather than getting on with their tasks? Is it that they fail to tidy up their work area at the end of the day? Or is it that they plod on and do the obvious without adapting to exceptions, or do not check their work and make lots of avoidable mistakes? These, and many more, could be different aspects of behaviour that singly or collectively amount to 'being lazy'. It is unlikely that someone is going to fall down on all these counts; some tendencies are going to be more prevalent than others. If we are to solve the problem, it is vital to be clear about the way or ways in which the laziness manifests itself. If you doubt this, imagine trying to fix a motor car where the problem is described as it will not go properly. Immediately we would need to ask questions and/or take it for a trial run in order to clarify such a vague description of the problem. Only when we had pin-pointed some specific ways in which it does not go properly would we be in a position to know what to do to solve the problem. Similarly, we do not know what to do to solve laziness until some specifics have been identified. As you might expect, therefore, the approach to solving people-problems expounded in the next chapter emphasizes the importance of focusing on specific behaviours rather than vague things to do with personality. There will be much more about how to make this distinction later on.

SNAG 2   ASSUMING THAT PEOPLE-PROBLEMS ARE CAUSED BY 'INTERNAL'
EVENTS SUCH AS ATTITUDES AND FEELINGS
Analysing problems correctly is more than half-way to solving them. Unfortunately, managers tend to analyse problems with 'things' much more rigorously than those with people. When we analyse, say, a problem with a malfunctioning machine, we tend to look systematically for cause-and-effect relationships. We assume that there is an observable, identifiable cause which is directly linked to the malfunction, and we go on searching, testing this and testing that, until we have diagnosed the problem correctly. We would think it very odd indeed if, rather than searching for cause and effect, a manager immediately condemned the machine, claiming it had been possessed by evil spirits. We would also be very puzzled if he claimed that the machine was 'bolshie' and 'didn't want to work today', or that it had some personality defect.

Inappropriate though this seems in the case of a malfunctioning machine, it is more or less exactly the way we proceed when analysing people-problems. Having observed the malfunction, we tend to attribute it to invisible, underlying causes analogous to spirits and poltergeists; we assume that the malfunction has been caused by internal things such as needs, motives, attitudes and feelings. This analysis brings us to a full stop. Just as there is nothing we can do to cure a machine possessed of evil spirits ('that's a job for an expert'), we are at a loss to know what to do to change needs, motives, attitudes and feelings.

Let us look more closely at internal explanations of people-problems.

Suppose, for example, that we have an employee who is consistently below par in his performance. The traditional approach would be to think of the poor performance as a symptom with an underlying cause. This way of thinking would inevitably mean that we would search for explanations for the poor performance by speculating about its internal causes. We may express the problem in a variety of ways: we may say that his needs are not being met or that his motives are incompatible with the job objectives; alternatively, we might say that he has not got the right attitude or that he is temperamentally unsuited to the work. The trouble with these explanations is that they sound very plausible but do not take us any farther forwards in thinking of an appropriate solution. What is a manager to *do* if someone has the wrong attitude? How can the manager change the employee's underlying needs and motives so that they are more compatible with the job to be done? What he will normally do is talk to the employee about the problem and attempt to persuade him to change these things himself. Unfortunately, the employee probably has no more idea how to change himself, even assuming that he wants to, than the manager. All too frequently, the result is that the problem persists and the manager becomes more and more desperate as each succeeding remonstration fails. Eventually, the manager may admit defeat, convinced that the employee has incurable personality defects.

The glib assumption that the poor performance was caused by internal factors has clouded the issue and prevented the manager from doing a thorough enough analysis of the problem. For example, the manager failed to think about *when* the behaviour occurs. Is the employee's performance always below par or are there times when it is better than others? Are there perhaps some tasks that the employee does less badly than others? And, from the employee's point of view, what does the poor performance lead to? Presumably there is some sort of pay-off for the employee in persisting which is stronger than the pep talks and disapproval of the manager? In short, the manager has failed to do a thorough diagnosis of the current situation and does not really deserve to solve the problem.

The widely held assumption that performance springs wholly from internal, underlying factors leads to three main difficulties for the practising manager. First, attributing external performance, or behaviour, to internal causes puts the problem-solving manager into a sort of cul-de-sac. Once he has decided the cause is a personality defect, where does he go from there? He is confronted with a series of dead ends; Figure 2.1 illustrates some popular ones.

Second, internal explanations complicate the issue to such an extent that a manager is likely to become impotent at solving people-problems. There is no need to postulate that behaviour is sometimes caused by underlying, internal events; there are always simpler, more straightforward explanations that avoid overwhelming the manager and save him from the problem-

13

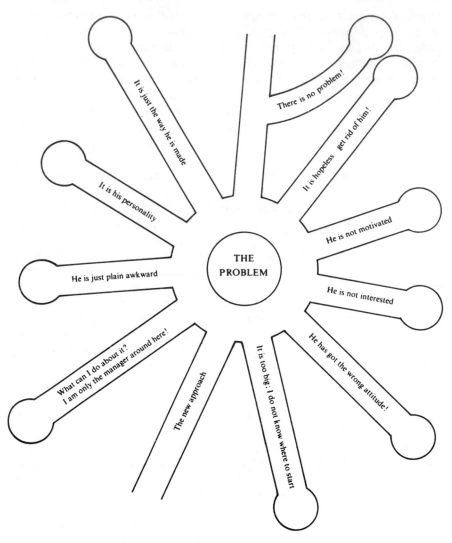

Figure 2.1

solving cul-de-sacs. Simpler explanations concentrate on the links between external happenings in the working environment and the way people are behaving or performing. Worries about underlying needs, motives, attitudes and feelings are left aside since they have less to contribute to either the analysis or the solution of the problem. This is not denying the existence of internal events, but rather claiming that they are less relevant than is usually supposed to the practising manager with people-problems to solve.

14

This brings us to the third point. Traditional internal explanations of people's performance at work tend to demand utopian heroics on the part of the manager. If people-problems have internal causes, it follows that the manager who hopes to solve them will have to delve deep in his attempt to understand inner motives, needs, feelings and attitudes. He will need to be a sensitive and empathic superman if he is to help each individual subordinate achieve their respective needs and feel satisfied. It is unlikely that professional psychologists, under carefully controlled conditions, could achieve such heroics. Whatever they say about psychologists, the busy practising manager is even less likely to succeed!

Thus, the traditional tendency to look for an internal explanation for poor performance or behaviour problems prevents the manager from doing a sound cause-and-effect diagnosis; it unnecessarily complicates the issue by introducing irrelevancies and demands that the manager wishing to diagnose and solve people-problems needs to be an empathic superman.

Despite all this, it is easy to understand why internal explanations are so popular. What happens is something like this: we each know through intro-spection that we experience feelings of guilt, joy, irritation, and so on. Often these feelings, which are internal, private experiences, tend to find outward expression in our behaviour; in this way we experience an apparent causal link between our underlying feelings and our behaviour or outward reactions. The association between the two events, internal and external, leads us to believe that the feelings caused the behaviour. In this way, we come to believe that, if we want to change someone's behaviour, we need to get to the 'root cause' and change their feelings.

There is another way of explaining these experiences that is both more helpful and more straightforward. Feelings and behaviour do not just happen in a vacuum; something in the external situation or environment triggers them. Feelings of guilt, joy and irritation are internal reactions to external stimuli. A subordinate misbehaves and we experience feelings of irritation. The monthly figures come in showing we have exceeded a tough target and we feel joyful. We are given credit for a piece of work done by one of our subordinates and we feel guilty. So behaviour is not caused by feelings; both internal feelings and external behaviour are reactions to external events. Sometimes we experience both in tandem, sometimes one without the other, but there is always an external happening that operates as a trigger.

Naturally, we shall be exploring this sort of explanation more fully, but notice the advantage it offers to the practising manager. Instead of wrestling with feelings in order to change behaviour, he now has a much more prac-ticable alternative. If something in the working environment has triggered the behaviour, he needs to identify what the external cause is and consider ways of changing it. If he changes the external trigger, he will be successful in changing the behaviour and he can leave underlying feelings to look after

15

themselves. This means that the manager's attention is quite properly focused on things that are observable and within his orbit to do something about. Managers are responsible for performance; arranging the environment so that performance is improved is exactly what a manager is supposed to do. The focus should be on performance pure and simple.

It is now time to describe the new approach and return to some of the people-problems posed in Chapter 1.

3. *A new approach to solving people-problems*

We have already seen that the new approach focuses on actual, observable behaviour rather than vague things like personality, attitudes and underlying feelings. This emphasis on behaviour itself provides the title of the approach —Behaviour Modification.

The advantage of this title is that it is descriptively accurate. We will see that the approach seeks to solve people-problems by quite literally working out how to modify the behaviour of the person or people involved. Its disadvantage is that you may find it rather off-putting, you may feel that it smacks of Big Brother or that it makes the approach sound ominously cold and calculating. If so, these initial reactions, though unwarranted, are quite understandable. Behaviour Modification *can* sound rather alarming, and consequently Chapter 8 is devoted exclusively to airing ethical considerations. Meanwhile, try to remember that the whole idea of the Behaviour Modification approach is to make things better for everyone involved: the other person, yourself and anyone else who might be affected by the problem. Remember we are trying to *solve* problems, not *make* them. Used appropriately, the approach aids the achievement of tasks, improves people's performance and enhances relationships between people.

Since Behaviour Modification is rather a mouthful, I will refer to it more simply throughout the rest of the book as BMod.

The BMod problem-solving approach has been adapted from the principles of clinical behaviour therapy and modification. In clinical settings these principles have been successful in solving some 'extreme' behavioural problems like phobias of various kinds, obesity and compulsive smoking. The same basic concepts can be successful in solving less dramatic problems encountered at work. What are the basic concepts? Basically there are three BMod 'buzz' words: behaviour, cue and pay-off. I will define each word separately before combining them into a problem-solving model. We shall start with behaviour itself; we have already met this word because it is the core of the BMod approach.

Behaviour

The word behaviour does not probably strike you as a piece of jargon. We need to dwell on its usage in the context of BMod, however, since in everyday parlance it does tend to get used in a moralistic, rather than dispassionate way. Parents often beg their children to behave themselves or ask that they be on their 'best' behaviour. At work we tend to talk about behaviour in terms associated with its goodness or badness: 'If he goes on behaving like that, he'll be for the high jump' and 'His behaviour left a lot to be desired.'

In BMod we need to use the word rather differently. Quite literally, behaviour refers to everything, good or bad, that people manifestly *do*. So the things that people *do* which are observable in a straightforward way we call behaviour. This obviously includes a vast range, the things people *say* in face-to-face situations as well as all the non-verbal actions people take. So whether people stand or sit, look or do not look, contribute or keep quiet, fidget or keep still, agree or disagree, answer questions or evade them, announce decisions or leave things open—all these are observable aspects of their behaviour.

Different behaviour is appropriate in different settings of course. Sometimes it is appropriate to keep quiet for instance; at other times it is inappropriate. This distinction between appropriate and inappropriate behaviour is important because in BMod we obviously need to concentrate on inappropriate behaviour—the type which gives rise to problems.

It is even more important to distinguish between actual behaviour and other closely associated aspects. As I tried to show in the last chapter, motives, attitudes and feelings all differ from behaviour in that they are not directly observable; they are internal events which may or may not manifest themselves in outward behaviour. You may *feel* irritated, for example, but manage not to *behave* it. Conversely, you may feel elated while displaying a cool, calm outward appearance. You may distrust (an attitude) people who have shifty eyes but conceal it in your dealings with (your behaviour) shifty-eyed people. So behaviour is *always* overt and observable; other aspects are by their very nature covert and unobservable.

Of course you may be quite skilled at *inferring* what people's motives, attitudes or feelings are, but you do this by observing their behaviour, reading between the lines as it were, and guessing the person's internal state. Sometimes this is fairly easy when someone 'blows their top', for example; at other times it is much more difficult. When someone is fairly deadpan it can be hazardous to jump to conclusions about their inner state. Many a seller has spoilt his presentation by doing that with a prospective buyer!

By now you may be feeling that all this emphasis on behaviour and whether it is observable or not is rather hair-splitting. In fact, there are two very good reasons for this emphasis on overt behaviour.

One is that BMod is an approach to solving problems caused by people's *behaviour*. It does not presume to go farther and modify people's personalities or to tamper with their underlying motives, attitudes or feelings. BMod, as the title suggests, concentrates on behaviour itself and seeks to modify it whenever it is detrimental to the achievement of objectives, the accomplishment of work tasks or relationships between people. Since behaviour is the centrepiece of the whole approach, it is hardly surprising that we should start by trying to be clear what behaviour actually is and distinguishing it from other associated, but different features.

The other reason for this emphasis is more practical; it is simply that, because behaviour is observable, we can be certain about it. Speculation is the best we can do about all the other attributes. So there is considerable advantage in concentrating on behaviour because at least we are tackling something we *know* about; it avoids getting stuck in a morass of underlying complications about motives, attitudes and feelings. As we saw in the last chapter, the approach does not deny the existence of these internal events, merely that, when it comes to solving people-problems, they unnecessarily complicate the issue.

Cues

Hopefully, the word cue is not going to cause too many problems. In BMod the word is used in exactly the same way as in a theatrical setting where a cue, usually a line or word of dialogue, triggers some action on or off the stage. This is exactly what happens with people's behaviour. In BMod a cue is any external event that triggers a behavioural reaction. Behaviour does not occur in a vacuum—people do not say and do things out of context. Some event (a cue) sets the conditions for a given piece of behaviour to occur. Here are some examples.

Suppose someone was persistently negative and this took the form of explaining why things could not be done. Traditional internal approaches would indicate that this behaviour was caused by underlying factors such as motives, attitudes and feelings, and that these must be changed if we are to succeed in modifying the negative behaviour. So the internal approach would regard the negative behaviour as a 'symptom' and try to solve the problem by going to the underlying cause. Typical internal explanations of the negative behaviour would be as follows:
- He is *feeling* threatened/inadequate.
- He is *motivated* to resist change.
- He *wants* to maintain the status quo.
- He has the wrong *attitude*.
- He is *biased* against changes.

As we saw in the last chapter, these explanations may or may not be the case. If we attribute the negative behaviour to causes like these, however, it is difficult to see how to proceed. Wrestling with underlying feelings, motives, wants, attitudes and biases is just too much to expect of us.

If we think of the negative behaviour in terms of cues, we can approach the problem quite differently. Now the negative behaviour is regarded as *the problem* rather than a mere symptom of another, deeper one. The external approach stresses that there must be something in the external environment

19

which is actively encouraging the negative behaviour and, furthermore, that if these external influences or cues can be pin-pointed, the behaviour could be modified by changing them and leaving the underlying motives, attitudes and feelings to look after themselves.

What sort of external events might be triggering negative behaviour? Remember that 'negative' is a word which encompasses many different behavioural reactions and nuances. Earlier we said it took the form of explaining why things cannot be done, so to identify the cues that are triggering this behaviour we need to ask ourselves, 'What is it that occurs *before* he explains why things can't be done?' The answer to this question will give us some likely cues. Typical answers might be when:
– suggestions for change come at him 'out of the blue';
– he is presented with a *fait accompli* with no consultation along the way;
– so-and-so makes the suggestion;
– the suggestion is put to him in a meeting with some of his subordinates present.

Now we are on to something! Instead of being overwhelmed with the sheer magnitude of internal explanations, we have identified some simple cues that may be triggering the negative behaviour. Admittedly we do not *know* that they are triggering the behaviour, but then we did not *know* that our speculations about the underlying motives, attitudes and feelings were right either. The cues we have pin-pointed, however, can be tested to check their validity. It would be quite easy to see if his behaviour is less negative when he is consulted, for example, or when the suggested change is made by someone else, or when it is put to him privately rather than in the presence of his subordinates.

Of course we do not have to test the validity of the cues we have identified unless we want to; the point is that we have the choice. Sometimes we might circumvent the business of actually checking out the accuracy of the cues by thinking of instances when our negative man had been less negative or even positive. Assuming he is not always negative on every occasion, this should not be too difficult. We could then try to work out what cued the less negative behaviour and contrast those cues with our former set. In this way we could check whether or not the cues we had identified made sufficient sense.

Aside from being testable, how do these cues help us to solve the problem? Well, if we are right and the events we have listed *do* in fact trigger the negative behaviour, then clearly we need to see if we can alter the existing cues and in consequence the behaviour. If we literally reversed the existing cues, for example, it seems highly likely that the negative behaviour would occur less often, if at all. Reversing the existing cues would mean that suggestions for change would no longer come at him 'out of the blue' and that he is never presented with a *fait accompli*. So clearly, in this instance, we need to be careful to consult with him and involve him at all stages in the change process. Furthermore, our analysis of the existing cues indicates that we need to be careful who does the suggesting of changes; it may well be that changes suggested from some quarters meet negative reactions and changes from others do not. And, finally, our cues indicate that suggestions for change must not be put to him 'in public', as it were, with his subordinates in attendance.

So being clear about the behaviour in question and what cues or external events seemed to trigger it was immediately fruitful in giving some feasible leads on how the behaviour could be modified. Change the cue and you change the behaviour.

Let us return to the people-problems in Chapter 1 and do a cue–behaviour analysis on them before moving on to look at pay-offs.

Turn back to the problem the husband had with his nagging wife on page 2 and, despite the scant description of the problem, see if you can identify the cue or cues.

According to the description of the problem, the main cue triggering the nagging is clearly something to do with the things about the house that need fixing. It is unlikely to be as straightforward as that, however; in real life the chances are that the nagging is triggered by extra cues such as:

- the husband arriving home late because he stopped off at the local for a drink with the boys;
- the wife having been seriously inconvenienced by something that needed fixing;
- the husband arriving home full of the joys of spring, saying what an interesting day he has had.

In the real-life situation, all these cues and others like them could easily be identified by the husband if he cared to think about it. Each cue that he pin-points makes it likely that he will be able to work out how to modify his wife's nagging in such a way that both partners benefit. This problem and the others described in Chapter 1 are dealt with further on pages 25–28.

Regarding Problem 2 on page 2 about the difficult shop steward, we need to be clear what cues the shop steward to burst into the personnel manager's office with unreasonable demands. Something must trigger this. Is it the time of day? Perhaps he always does it just before lunch, just after lunch, or at the end of the day shift. Does he do it every day? What events occur on the days when he does do it that do not occur, or are substantially different, on the days when he does not do it? Is there a pattern or does the shop steward behave like this on an entirely random basis?

The personnel manager found there *was* a pattern. Once he escaped from the dead end of assuming that the shop steward was just plain awkward, he began to distinguish between the times when the shop steward was absurdly demanding and aggressive and the times when he was less so. It transpired

21

that he was particularly overdemanding when he was representing a small group of workers in just one unit of the shop floor; he was less demanding when he was representing other groups on the same shop floor. This discovery about the cue led the personnel manager to other insights about the shop steward's behaviour. It was not long before he had a strategy that succeeded in making the shop steward more reasonable in his demands.

In Problem 3 on page 2, Ron was peeved because his boss was circumventing him. Ron attributed the blame for this to his boss, and concluded that the circumvention was deliberate. Looking at it this way was cosy for Ron and absolved him from further responsibilities in the matter. After all, if the boss was *deliberately* circumventing him, it was unfortunate and Ron would wish it otherwise, but what can he *do* other than grin and bear it? Well, one very useful thing he can do is set to work and identify some cues. He needs to ask himself questions like these:

- 'What happens *before* my boss circumvents me that appears to trigger it?'
- 'Does he *always* circumvent me or are there instances of his searching me out and consulting with me?'
- 'On what sort of issues does he circumvent me?'
- 'Is there any difference between these issues and the issues where there is consultation between us?'

In real life Ron was encouraged to address the problem by asking these questions. In no time at all he discovered something about his boss's behaviour that had not previously dawned on him—there *was* a pattern. His boss consistently circumvented Ron on all issues where he knew (or thought he knew) from past experience that Ron would prove an obstacle and hamper the action he wanted to take; on issues where it was likely that Ron would be supportive, the boss consulted him. Now, of course, this discovery does not on its own solve the problem; maybe Ron does not fancy becoming a yes-man. It does give Ron something to work on, however. In real life Ron solved the problem and succeeded in modifying this aspect of his boss's behaviour. There is more about how he did that on pages 27–28.

You might now like to try your hand at spotting the cues in the remaining three problems described in Chapter 1; they are on pages 3–5. In each case you should be able to do two things:

1. Pin-point a specific, observable behaviour that is proving a disappointment to the person with the problem.
2. Identify a cue, or cues, that appear to be triggering the behaviour in question.

I shall return to these three cases in the next chapter and you will be able to compare your analysis with the way the problems were solved in real life by using the BMod approach.

Pay-offs

In the BMod approach, pay-offs are even more significant than cues in solving people-problems. Strictly speaking, a pay-off is the climax of a dramatic situation or story. In BMod we use the expression to refer to what happens *after* the behaviour that is a satisfactory outcome *for the person behaving*; the pay-off is the 'climax' that follows or results from the behaviour.

Pay-offs are an absolutely vital ingredient in the BMod problem-solving approach. As we have seen, the identification of cues often results in breakthroughs giving fresh insights into what could be done to modify an undesirable behaviour. The insights that result from looking at pay-offs are just as important, and often even more crucial, in developing a solution to the problem.

Why are pay-offs so important? It is because cues tell only half the story—people do not merely react to events and happenings like machines or lesser animals do. People *learn* as a result of their experiences and this means they develop the ability to anticipate an outcome from their behaviour. This is fundamental to the way we bring up our children. A new-born baby cries (behaviour) when hungry (a cue); initially that is a cue giving rise to a behaviour in an utterly mechanical way, just as turning the ignition key in a car is a cue for the engine to start. Unlike the car, however, the baby starts to learn from the sequence of events. After a while the baby puts two and two together. If babies could verbalize, the reasoning would be something like this: 'When I have the unpleasant experience of being alone or feeling hungry, I cry. This attracts attention. I get picked up and fondled; I get fed; I am amused and made comfortable. I like all these things. Much better than lying here all alone. I'll cry and enjoy the pay-offs.' Of course babies are not able to express such a sequence of events in this way but they cotton on to the links between cues, behaviour and pay-offs all the same! In effect, repeated patterns of events build up connections between them and, in no time at all, a mechanical, reflex action (crying) is modified and used as a way of securing pay-offs. The fact that this still happens without the ability to reason underlines the vital role that pay-offs play in the acquisition of behaviour patterns. It does not matter whether the behaviour is good or bad, desirable or undesirable. All that matters is that it works!

The BMod argument is, therefore, that all our behaviour is indulged in not merely in reaction to events (cues) but also in anticipation of some outcome (pay-offs). So if we want to modify someone's behaviour, we need to know about its pay-offs as well as its cues.

I shall illustrate this by returning to the problem of the negative man who frequently explained why things could not be done. In the last section we isolated some cues that appeared to trigger this behaviour; as we saw, cues always happen *before* the behaviour. Now we need to look at what happens *after* the behaviour that is an encouraging consequence or outcome for the person.

So, in the case of the negative man, we need to ask: 'What is it that happens *after* he has explained why things can't be done that appears to be a satisfactory outcome (pay-off) for him?' Answers to this question might be:
- On a high percentage of occasions his resistance wins the day (causes the proposed changes to be dropped or significantly lessened).
- The proposers pay attention to him.
- People congratulate him for being a stickler.
- He avoids having to change anything or at least minimizes the things he has to change.
- He gets himself into a position where he can say 'If things go wrong, don't blame me. I've warned you.'
- His subordinates show that they admire the way he protects/represents them.

Now we have the whole picture. We can see, much as we may not welcome it, why the man is negative—not only is the behaviour triggered by certain events, it is also clear that it is very advantageous to the negative man. For him there is every advantage in his behaving in this way. In short, the behaviour results in pay-offs for our negative man and, while this state of affairs continues, so will his negative behaviour. As surely as babies cry for attention, our man will react negatively when people propose changes to him.

So what is to be done about it? Do we admit defeat? Are we stuck with a negative man? Certainly not. We have already seen how the analysis of the cues that triggered the behaviour gave us ideas on how events could be rearranged to discourage the negative reaction. Now we have something to work on at the other end, *after* the behaviour has occurred. The pay-offs give us a whole host of possible actions.

For example, the discovery that his resistance wins the day and causes proposed changes to be dropped or lessened means that we could be careful to ensure that this outcome only occurs when he has been positive and not when he has been negative. This would be a reversal of the current state of affairs. So when he is negative there are no concessions; it is only when he is less negative that he gets the pay-off. This means that, when he suggests modifications to the proposed changes, he is rewarded by winning the day. However, when he blocks any modifications, the reaction is such that he loses the day.

If this reversal of the usual pattern of events was repeated on a number of occasions, we would expect to see the man become less negative and more positive in the face of change. If you couple this pay-off strategy with the

24

ideas we had earlier about altering the cues, then it is very likely indeed that the problem of negative behaviour has been overcome. The combination of cues and pay-offs is enormously potent. The altered cues make it less likely that the negative behaviour will occur in the first place; when it does, the altered pay-offs ensure that there is no longer any advantage in it—quite the reverse, in fact. There is now every advantage in being positive.

The other pay-offs we listed could be built into the strategy in a similar way; they all have a contribution to make. For example, one pay-off that resulted from his negative behaviour was that the proposers paid attention to him. In future, the proposers would need to be careful to pay more attention to him when he was positive and less when he was negative. Another pay-off was that people congratulated him for being a stickler. Well, now it must be arranged so that the accolades come congratulating him for improving the proposed changes.

Now let us return once more to the people-problems described in Chapter 1. We have already looked in each case at the cues triggering the behaviour. Now we can complete the picture by looking at pay-offs.

The husband with the wife who nagged him when things about the house needed maintenance. Why is she nagging? What pay-offs does this behaviour result in? The answer is plain to see—the nagging is successful in getting results. The husband may grumble, but no doubt the wife has discovered that there is an association between her nagging and the things getting done. It is unlikely that she has consciously thought this through and, without the benefit of BMod, it is most unlikely that the husband has either. The fact is that the wife has learned that the way to get her husband to do these routine chores is to nag him until he submits; when she does not nag him, he just postpones the tasks. Only nagging does the trick. It may well be that the wife resents having to nag; on the other hand, she may get some sort of satisfaction out of doing it. Whether she enjoys it or not, however, is irrelevant. Much more significant is that she has found it is a strategy that gets results.

So we have an interesting paradox: unwittingly the husband has been actively encouraging behaviour in his wife that he does not like. He may blame his wife and assume that 'It's just the way she's made'. We can now see that he has been doing all the right things to aid and abet the nagging. The solution to this problem is in his own hands. What can he do to solve it?

The first thing he must do after pin-pointing the existing cues and pay-offs surrounding the nagging behaviour is to decide what behaviour he wants in its place. This may seem obvious—you would probably suggest he goes for 'no nagging'. However, this presents a problem. It is not as easy to eradicate a behaviour and leave a vacuum as it is to replace it with a more desirable behaviour.

25

'No nagging' is a description of something the wife would not do; it does not positively describe something the husband wants her to do instead of nagging. So it requires a little thought. In real life the husband decided that the behaviour he wanted to replace the nagging with was that his wife just asked him once. This is a more feasible behaviour to go for. It gives him something positive to work on and is more specific than simply saying 'no nagging'. After all, what is no nagging? If you think about it, you will see that it *is* asking just once without any repetitions of the same request.

So the husband wants to replace nagging with asking once. Can he change any of the existing cues? Unlikely, since something will have to cue being asked once and, in all probability, it will be the fact that the wife notices things about the house that need fixing. Of course, the husband could be careful (especially when he has had a 'good' day at the office) to *enquire* if things need fixing. This would trigger the first request and may make it less likely that nagging would ensue.

You may be thinking of another obvious strategy for the husband. What about preventive maintenance? If the nagging is triggered by the sight of such things as taps dripping and pelmets hanging off the wall, then is it not obvious that the way to avoid all this is to fix taps *before* they drip and to secure pelmets *before* they become loose? Well, the answer is no for two reasons. Firstly, if the husband did his preventive maintenance well enough, then the behaviour he desires (being asked just once) is unlikely to occur. If it does not occur, then he cannot encourage it over and above the tendency to nag. Secondly, preventive maintenance is unrealistic; it is unlikely that the husband could keep up with the schedule it would entail even if he wanted to! In BMod we look for solutions to problems which are adequate and, above all, feasible. If it is not feasible, it cannot be kept to; if it cannot be kept to, perhaps over long periods while the old behaviour diminishes and the new one strengthens, then it is not going to work.

So suppose the husband actually asks his wife what things need his attention (the new cue) and she replies by telling him about the dripping bathroom tap. What now? Is that all there is to it? Certainly not. The most important part is yet to come. The husband must now work out what he needs to do *after* she has asked him. He needs to work out what pay-off to use to encourage being asked once and how to discourage the old nagging behaviour. If you remember, we decided that the nagging was unwittingly being encouraged when the husband succumbed and fixed things; this was the wife's pay-off for nagging. How can the husband rearrange things so that she gets her pay-offs by asking just once?

Easily. Immediately after his wife has told him about something that needs fixing, the husband whips out his diary, goes exactly 10 days ahead and says 'I will fix that on such-and-such a date. But if you repeat the request in the intervening period, I'm afraid I'll have to put the date back a further 10

26

days.' If she does not nag, he fixes whatever it is on the agreed day; that is his part of the bargain. In doing so he is ensuring that his wife gets a satisfactory pay-off—the item is fixed without any 'aggro'. If she does nag, the job is postponed. So now the wife's previous advantage in nagging has been replaced with an advantage in asking once. Things get fixed sooner than under the old system; the wife is pleased. The husband now fixes the things he previously fixed but without all the resentments associated with nagging. Everyone gains and the problem is solved.

Of course there may be some hiccups along the way. What if something more urgent crops up so that the husband cannot keep his promise to fix the dripping tap on the designated date? The answer is that he must apologize and fix the tap slightly earlier than he said he would. In the circumstances this is the least he can do, and the vital thing is that he must avoid a relapse into nagging behaviour by doing anything to jeopardize the new behaviour. He must stick to his side of the deal come what may. The rewards will be worth it.

What about the personnel manager and the 'stroppy' shop steward? How does the pay-off part of the analysis help in solving this problem? Well, it rather echoes the husband-and-wife problem (as so many work problems do). Over the years the personnel manager and the factory management had unwittingly granted more concessions when the shop steward was over-demanding than they had when he was reasonable. This had had the inevitable effect of increasing the unreasonable behaviour (since it was found to work) and reducing the reasonable behaviour in the shop steward. Once this was realized, the key to solving the problem was in the personnel manager's hands. He had to ensure that reasonable behaviour was rewarded with pay-offs and that unreasonable behaviour was not. Easy. Ensure that more concessions occur from reasonable demands and less from unreasonable ones.

Ah, you say, that would have them in dire trouble in no time! Strikes would increase, productivity would drop, relations between employees and management would be strained to breaking point. Not so. Throughout the transitional period, strikes remained the same; they neither increased nor decreased. The cost of the concessions did not increase either. It is just that concessions shifted from being made when the shop steward was unreasonable to when he was reasonable. Overall the magnitude of the concessions remained much the same; the factor that changed dramatically was the shop steward's behaviour. Over a three-monthly period, the impossible happened —he became increasingly more reasonable. Nothing was lost, everything was gained.

Finally, let us look at the problem Ron had with his boss. What pay-offs were operating there? If you remember, Ron had realized that his boss circumvented him when he suspected that Ron was going to thwart him; he

27

consulted him only when the topics were likely to secure Ron's support. So pay-offs for Ron's boss must have been associated with getting his own way while avoiding an uncomfortable (for the boss) confrontation.

Once again, we see that the key to modifying the boss's behaviour is in Ron's hands. If he initiates consultation (a changed cue) with his boss and is careful to reward this by largely agreeing rather than disagreeing, then consultation will increase. If he persists in being difficult (from the boss's point of view), circumvention will increase. The choice is Ron's since his behaviour has proved so crucial in shaping that of his boss. Even when Ron is honour bound to disagree with his boss (on matters of principle), he could find ways of doing so that cushioned adverse effects and avoided driving the boss away. He could, for example, add to the boss's ideas rather than being entirely negative. In this way, he might succeed in modifying both the ideas and the boss's behaviour! Two birds with one stone cannot be bad.

Now try your hand at identifying pay-offs in the remaining three people-problems described in Chapter 1. What were the pay-offs for Ian in adopting such an aggressive style? What pay-offs was Ted's director enjoying at Ted's expense? And, finally, what was in it for Maureen when she failed to process the vouchers by the deadline?

In each case you should be able to identify pay-offs that were powerful enough to encourage the continuance of the behaviour of the 'guilty parties'. In doing so, remember that behaviour does not just happen by accident; it is initiated by both cues and pay-offs. The secret is to identify both and work out how to change them in the interests of modifying the behaviour sandwiched in between. Sometimes you may be able to think of ways of changing both cues and pay-offs; in other cases you may only be able to think of changes to the pay-offs. Either way you will be able to compare your solutions with those described in the next chapter.

The BMod problem-solving model

As we have seen, BMod sets out basically to pin-point three things. If you imagine that person A wants to modify person B's behaviour, they are:
1. A specific behaviour exhibited by B that is undesirable because it is detrimental to B's overall performance.
2. The external events that cue or trigger this behaviour in B.
3. The pay-off the behaviour results in for B.
This gives us a simple model as shown in Figure 3.1.

The BMod approach initially concentrates on analysing problems by identifying the links between these three. It then goes on to produce a strategy to solve the problem by working out:
4. What specific behaviour is desirable in the light of the problem A has with B.

5. How existing cues can be changed to make the desirable behaviour more likely in B and the undesirable behaviour less likely.
6. How B's existing pay-offs can be changed so that the desirable behaviour is encouraged and/or the undesirable behaviour discouraged.

There are some complications to sort out in subsequent chapters, but basically that is how to solve people-problems using BMod.

At the end of the first chapter I encouraged you to think of a couple of your own people-problems. Now is the time to see if you can solve them using the BMod approach. By going through the above six steps you should be able to arrive at feasible solutions which have not previously occurred to you.

Figure 3.1

4. *Solving people-problems successfully*

In this chapter I am going to show how the BMod approach was successful in solving three people-problems described in Chapter 1. The three problems are: Ian, the managing director (pages 3–4), Overloaded Ted (pages 4–5), and Bert, the supervisor (page 5).

You may have already done some work on these during the last chapter when we were looking at cues and pay-offs; if so, you will be able to compare your analysis and solutions with the ones given in this chapter. This is not to suggest that there are 'textbook' answers to these or any other people-problems—quite the contrary, there will be many equally viable alternative solutions. However, one interesting thing about the solutions given in this chapter is that they were the actual solutions arrived at using BMod and successfully implemented in real life.

I am conscious that this is a 'make-or-break' chapter in advancing the BMod cause; earlier chapters have merely paved the way for this one. By the end of this chapter I want to have convinced you that BMod is a successful way of solving people-problems. As I have said already, BMod is a no-nonsense, pragmatic approach and, as such, it must stand or fall by its ability to come up with viable solutions and to succeed where other approaches have failed.

Ian, the managing director

If you remember, Ian was the young, hard-working MD whose management style was very unpopular with his direct reports! He was enormously suspicious of their competence, pounced and sorted out their problems for them, ran divisive problem-solving meetings, and kept everyone fearful of being caught without all the facts at their fingertips. Rick, the personnel director, was particularly concerned about the adverse consequences of Ian's behaviour. He noticed that his colleague directors were becoming more cautious, more bogged down in detail, more competitive and less open about mistakes and inadequacies. In view of this, Rick decided to modify Ian's behaviour.

I have given this particular problem to hundreds of managers and asked them:
1. What is the problem?
2. What advice would you give to Rick about how to solve the problem?
Here are the usual answers to these questions. Remember that these answers

are given *before* the managers know anything about the BMod approach.

The problem is usually described loosely as 'Ian's style'. When pressed, this is expanded to 'Ian's autocratic style'.

The traditional solutions, in order of popularity, are as follows:

Solution 1   Rick should have a session with Ian where he finds out why Ian is adopting such an autocratic style, and points out what a disastrous effect it is having on everybody.

This idea is usually supported by people who have noticed that Ian has 'complained to Rick' about the directors' behaviour. It is taken as an encouraging sign that Ian himself has begun to see the error of his ways and is, therefore, likely to welcome Rick's initiative.

Solution 2   Rick must persuade Ian and his directors to go off on a residential weekend together.

The advantage of this idea is claimed to be that it will get them out of the normal work place and give them long enough together to sort out relationship problems. The weekend would take the form of a workshop and there are usually vague notions about hiring an outside consultant to come and do 'something about management styles' with the group.

Solution 3   Rick must persuade his colleague directors to have a show-down with Ian the next time he behaves autocratically in a meeting.

This is a sort of 'palace revolution' formula, and managers who propound it look noticeably sheepish as they do so! The idea is that the next time Ian is nasty to his directors, collectively and to a man, they will confront him with his nastiness and refuse to cooperate. 'Enough is enough. We'll kowtow no more!'

Solution 4   Rick must complain about Ian's behaviour and its effects to Ian's boss.

The idea is deliberately to escalate the problem by bypassing Ian and

31

in effect smuggle a message out to the MD of the group to which Ian's company reports. This solution is supported by people who feel that Ian's subordinates are powerless to make any impact on a tyrant such as Ian. There is nothing for it but to appeal higher up the hierarchy.

> Solution 5   Rick must have a session with Ian where he tries to clarify Ian's objectives and how he views the objectives of his directors.

This is a sort of 'management by objectives' approach. Its supporters argue that a debate about objectives will provide a more fruitful foothold for tackling the real issue of Ian's management style than addressing the problems head-on.

> Solution 6   Rick must take the initiative by suggesting a more formal structure for the meetings.

The idea behind this solution is to prevent meetings with Ian degenerating into inquisitions. The philosophy here is to let the structure take the strain and arrange things so that it muffles Ian and prevents his unseemly outbursts. A radical idea often mooted in this connection is that the agreed structure could allow for someone other than Ian to be in the chair.

> Solution 7   Rick must search out a friend of Ian's and, if such a person exists, get him to do the 'dirty work' by confronting Ian with the consequences of his style.

I expect this solution would be more popular if people could imagine Ian having any friends!

> Solution 8   Rick must help his colleague directors come to terms with Ian's behaviour.

The line would be: 'For the immediate future we are stuck with Ian. We'll just have to grin and bear it. After all, it can't last for ever!'

So we have eight different ideas about how the problem could be solved. Of course there is merit in many of these ideas, and some of them sound quite plausible. Confronting Ian with the consequences of his style may well shock him into making modifications. Getting him away on a weekend workshop or approaching the problem via job clarification and objective setting are also attractive ideas, since they avoid outright confrontation and may provide eye-openers for Ian. Nothing would be lost by trying some of these ideas to see if they had the desired effect. If they did, there would be no need to use BMod.

I personally feel, however, that none of the proposed solutions is likely to provide a permanent solution to the problem. This is because:

1. The problem has not been pin-pointed precisely enough.
2. The factors in the situation that are triggering and sustaining Ian's behaviour have not been identified. While these remain, so will Ian's behaviour.

So how does BMod help to give more worthwhile advice to Rick about how he could solve the problem?

Firstly, the BMod approach requires him to do a much more thorough job on the analysis of the problem. It is too much of a platitude to claim that the problem is 'Ian's style' or even 'Ian's *autocratic* style'. It is fine to talk loftily about autocratic styles at an abstract level, but it will not get us off to a good start in solving this problem. For one thing, it does not begin to pin-point what the problem actually is. An autocratic style is not necessarily a problem; there are countless situations where such a style is admirable and quite the best way to get the desired results. Even more important, however, is that if the problem is described in such an inexact way, it makes it extremely difficult to identify *when* the style occurs, and this is vital as a starting point in a BMod analysis. It may be that Ian consistently adopts an autocratic *style* but that it manifests itself in different ways from situation to situation. If he *always* uses an autocratic style, we will be at a loss to see what triggers it and, if we cannot identify cues, then we have drawn a blank with at least half of the BMod formula. If, however, we break down his autocratic style and pin-point the behaviour he actually uses, we are much more likely to be able to discover revealing patterns between certain events (cues) and the way Ian reacts (behaviour).

Let us use BMod principles to pin-point the problem, analyse the existing situation and come up with a plausible, lasting solution.

The first step is to identify a specific behaviour that is undesirable because it is detrimental to Ian's overall performance. A good way to arrive at this is to start by listing all the actions that Ian takes that are likely to be seen as problems by Rick. If the list is long, when we can help Rick to whittle it down by selecting the behaviour that he judges to be the *most detrimental* to Ian's performance as managing director. Here is what the list would look like:

– His meetings are like inquisitions.
– He is a stickler for detail.

– He sends people scurrying for facts.
– He adopts an aggressive questioning style.
– He bawls people out in public.
– He interferes a great deal.
– He pounces on and sorts out problems himself.
– He complains about the fire-fighting tendency in his subordinate directors.
– He cannot understand why people think he is a hard man.
– He has firm ideas on how best to manage.
– He expects people to work as hard as he does.
– He believes that people respond to pressure.

You might have some more things on the list, but there is already plenty for Rick to choose from. If he is wise in making his selection, he will reject the last four items on the grounds that they are not actually describing something Ian *does*. They are more to do with Ian's ideas, beliefs and expectations than they are to do with his outward behaviour. The essence of the BMod approach is that we are seeking to modify Ian's *behaviour*, not his attitudes or beliefs. If we are successful in modifying his behaviour, it may have a knock-on effect on his underlying attitudes and beliefs. The point is that BMod tackles overt behaviour first and foremost, not covert underlying factors. Rick should also reject the first item on the list. This is because it describes vividly but generally what the meetings are like and does not pin-point specific aspects of Ian's behaviour.

So Rick is left with six behaviours. He now needs to select just *one* of them for processing through the remaining steps; he must do this because BMod can only process one behaviour at a time. You can only put one coin at a time in the slot of a fruit machine, but this does not prevent you from hitting the jackpot! Similarly, BMod will only accept one behaviour at a time (and hits the jackpot more frequently than a fruit machine does!) The one-behaviour-at-a-time rule is a limiting factor but is necessary because different behaviours are associated with different cues and pay-offs. Just as one coin needs to journey right through a fruit machine before it is ready to accept the next, so one behaviour needs to be progressed through the BMod routine before it can cope with another. In Chapter 8 I shall discuss this and show that this factor is not such a handicap as it might appear.

As he has to make a choice, which of the remaining six behaviours on the list should Rick select? We should advise him to take the behaviour that he considers most detrimental to Ian's performance as managing director. In this context, we are obviously focusing attention on Ian's performance as a manager of a number of subordinate directors; we know from the description of the problem that Ian's tendency to wade in and sort out problems himself is having unwanted effects on their behaviour. It explains how Rick has noticed signs of stress, an increase in competitive behaviour and increasing preoccupation with matters of detail.

Since the six remaining behaviours were obviously closely linked, Rick decided to select 'He pounces and sorts out problems himself' as the most pressing behavioural problem. So let us take that one, but in doing so I want to stress that the BMod approach will come up with a potential solution for every behaviour on the list. It is not a question of taking an easy option.

With the problem behaviour selected, the next step in the BMod approach is to pin-point what external events cue or trigger this behaviour in Ian. So the question is: 'What happens *before* Ian "pounces and sorts out problems himself" that appears to trigger it?' The answer is in the text (it would hardly have been fair to omit it!). At the end of the first paragraph (on page 3) it says, 'As soon as he suspects a deficiency, he pounces and sorts it out himself.' The cue seems to be 'as soon as Ian suspects a deficiency'. If we read on we can see more precisely the sort of deficiencies that cause Ian to swing into action. It talks about problems to be solved and Ian's ability to 'move heaven and earth to fix problems'; we also know that the directors have a tendency to keep problems from Ian. It does not take too much imagination to realize that we have an interesting vicious circle here—the more the directors try to conceal and cover up problems, the more Ian is likely to be suspicious. We have now identified a link between Ian being suspicious and his 'pouncing'. By keeping information from him and attempting to cover up mistakes, the directors are unwittingly indulging in behaviour that *increases* the likelihood of Ian's pouncing with his inquisitions, his bawling them out in public, the lot! A BMod analysis often exposes paradoxes like this.

So now we have a cue and a behaviour as in Figure 4.1.

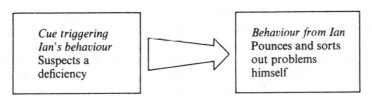

Figure 4.1

This is much more helpful in clarifying the problem (a far cry from it being 'Ian's autocratic style') but it is only half the story. We now need to identify pay-offs. If you remember, the BMod argument is that Ian must be employing his pouncing behaviour because he has found that it works. Despite his complaints about being misunderstood, his behaviour must be yielding the results he desires, otherwise he would abandon it and do something else. So, from Ian's point of view, what is it that happens after he has pounced and sorted out the problem himself that is a satisfactory outcome (pay-off)?

35

We do not have to look very far for some convincing answers to this question. At the end of the second paragraph (page 3) it says: 'Eventually he succeeds in solving the problem and in getting advance warning about other problems in the pipeline.' Here is his pay-off. It all adds up: we know Ian prides himself on his problem-solving ability, so the chances are he *enjoys* the drama of it all. That, though, is speculating about an *internal* pay-off— the *feeling* which Ian enjoys. Irrespective of whether Ian gets a kick out of solving problems his directors could not, there is a clear external pay-off: problems get fixed with the added bonus that, in the process, Ian uncovers more problems to get his teeth into. From Ian's point of view, there is every advantage in his pouncing behaviour; it does not matter how many people remonstrate with him, the behaviour will remain while it is sustained by such a powerful pay-off.

The full picture can now be shown in Figure 4.2.

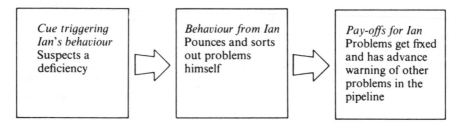

Figure 4.2

Armed with this analysis of the current situation, Rick stands an excellent chance of cracking the problem; both cue and pay-off give him a strong foothold. Do you see how inadequate earlier suggestions were? Rick and his colleagues would stand very little chance of making any *lasting* impact on Ian by having a show-down or by pointing out to Ian the consequences of his behaviour; he knows the consequences only too well and they suit him fine. Of course, there is a slender chance that the weekend workshop (*if* they could persuade Ian it was a worthwhile investment of the time) would have a temporary effect. He might be brought to realize that his pouncing had some undesirable side-effects. If so, in all probability he would want the best of both worlds: to continue to pounce but to water it down so that people did not take such umbrage. This compromise would soon frustrate him, particularly if, as seems likely, being nicer to people slowed down the problem solving. After a while the pay-off would predominate and Ian would return to his old ways.

So what is the BMod solution? To devise one, Rick needs to do three things:

1. Decide what new behaviour he wishes to see Ian using in place of the old one.
2. See if the existing cues give him ideas on how the new behaviour might be triggered.
3. See if the existing pay-offs give him ideas on how the new behaviour might be reinforced.

First we need to encourage Rick to be as clear about the behaviour he wants to see in Ian as he was in pin-pointing his disappointments. What specific behaviour does Rick think is desirable instead of 'pouncing and sorting out the problems himself'? Clearly, Rick has a choice here; he could go for a complete reversal 'not pouncing and not sorting out problems himself', but, as we have seen, this is difficult to achieve because it describes something Ian would no longer do and is not adequate in describing what he *would* do. Suppose Rick was successful in preventing Ian's pouncing—what would he do in the vacuum? Sit and twiddle his thumbs? Clearly that would not be desirable. We need to find a productive way of harnessing his energy and undoubted problem-solving abilities.

It would be much more satisfactory if Rick could identify something positive that he wanted Ian to do in the place of pouncing. Suppose he settled for 'helping people to solve their own problems'. This would be dramatically different from the current 'pouncing and sorting out problems himself'. 'Helping people to solve their own problems' is still a bit vague, however; what would Ian have to *do* that would amount to 'helping'? In this case, appropriate behaviours would be for Ian to:

– go through the pros and cons of alternative courses of action;
– develop other people's ideas on how the problem might be solved;
– ask questions that steer people with problems to discovering sound solutions for themselves.

So now we are clear on what would constitute 'helping' in this context. We are nearly there! All we have got to do now is concentrate on how to change the cues and pay-offs.

Back to cues. What could Rick do to make it likely that 'helping' was triggered instead of 'pouncing'? The old cue could give him a useful lead; if pouncing occurs whenever Ian suspected deficiencies, cover-ups and the like, how could this be changed to reduce pouncing and increase helping? Well, Rick could try out a simple experiment.

Suppose he goes to Ian with a substantial problem and asks Ian to help him solve it. The problem must be substantial, not trivial, and 'worthy' of Ian's attention. It should also be a relatively new problem, not something that has festered over a long period. The helping reaction is more likely to be triggered if Rick has data about the problem at his fingertips and has thought through a number of alternative solutions. In effect, therefore, he is asking Ian to help him weigh up the alternatives and settle on the best solution.

37

From what we know of Ian, this should be precisely his cup of tea. He prides himself on his abilities in this sphere, and so the fact that Rick voluntarily comes to him with a substantial new problem asking for help is likely to elicit a favourable response. At last, someone has recognized his problem-solving abilities, has brought a problem to him at an early stage instead of concealing it, and has come properly briefed, versed in all the ins and outs of the problem and with alternative solutions thought out. We can imagine Ian positively beaming and settling down to help with all the gusto that he previously invested in pouncing.

You doubt that such a revolutionary change could occur in Ian? You are probably right. It is more likely that Rick's experiment will make *some* headway in the right direction; Ian may be *more* helpful than usual in these circumstances but his tendency to grab the problem and solve it himself will probably still be much in evidence. Rick must be patient. Any progress towards helpful behaviour *is* progress. After all, Ian has probably acquired the pouncing behaviour over a long period, so replacing it with a new set of behaviours will take time. BMod is not magic—you cannot expect to wave a wand over Ian and completely transform him.

Having decided on a new behaviour and thought of a new cue we are half-way towards a feasible solution, as is shown in Figure 4.3.

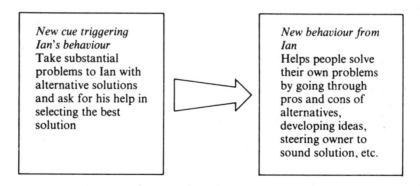

Figure 4.3

The final step is to consider Ian's pay-offs. We have already identified a number of pay-offs that seemed particularly important in sustaining the old pouncing behaviour. Inevitably, therefore, pay-offs are going to have to figure as an important feature in any attempt to modify Ian's behaviour. Besides the internal pay-offs that we suspected Ian experienced as a result of one of his problem-solving binges (feelings of self-satisfaction, feeling that he had demonstrated his superiority, etc.), our analysis showed that the external pay-off was that the problems got fixed with the additional benefit of advance warning of other problems in the pipeline.

We know as certainly as we know anything about Ian that these are important outcomes for him. This being so, Rick should now be careful to ensure that Ian gets his pay-offs after he has been helpful and is to some extent thwarted in getting them after he has pounced. On the face of it, Rick could arrange this quite easily; when Ian indulges in the helpful behaviours, Rick should be careful to behave supportively, efficiently, crisply and gratefully. It is vital that Ian gets his pay-offs, that the problem is fixed quickly and that he is furnished with the information he craves. On the other hand, when Ian pounces and solves the problem himself, Rick must be relatively less supportive, less efficient, less crisp and less grateful. The problem must be fixed less well and less quickly and Ian must finish up with less information about other problems in the pipeline.

You may find it difficult or even distasteful to envisage Rick *deliberately* thwarting Ian in any way; in practice, however, these are likely to be fairly 'natural' reactions to Ian when he pounces and not requiring a lot of conscious effort. It is highly likely that Rick and his colleagues already tend to react in relatively downtrodden, resentful ways when Ian pounces. To some extent they have already adopted uncooperative stances. The strategy allows for these natural reactions to continue, but in stark contrast to the way they react when Ian is helpful. When it comes to a conscious investment of effort, it is much more important that Rick rewards Ian when he is helpful than it is to thwart him when he is unhelpful. The whole strategy depends on Ian discovering that it pays to behave helpfully rather than not. This contrast can best be achieved if Rick works at accentuating the positive; in this way, Rick positively encourages Ian to be helpful and relatively discourages him from pouncing. Now things are rearranged so that Ian more easily achieves pay-offs by being helpful and less easily achieves them by pouncing.

Rick now has a carefully thought out strategy to implement, as illustrated in Figure 4.4.

If Rick sticks to this strategy, it is predictable that Ian's pouncing will decrease and his repertoire of helpful behaviours will increase. As I admitted earlier, this may take a little time, even weeks or months; exactly *how* long depends on the extent to which Ian's pouncing behaviour is ingrained and habitual and how often Rick can use the new cue. Obviously, it is no good going to Ian with trumped-up problems; they must be authentic and substantial enough to involve him.

After Rick has tested out this strategy and found it works, he can 'tip off' his fellow directors and encourage them to adopt a similar strategy. If it is successful, everyone gains: Ian gets his pay-offs faster and more frequently than before; the directors get help with their problems and stand to learn

New cue triggering Ian's behaviour
Take substantial problems to Ian
with alternative solutions and ask
for his help in selecting the
best solution

New behaviour from Ian
Helps people solve their own
problems by going through pros
and cons of alternatives,
developing ideas, steering
owner to sound solution, etc.

New pay-offs for Ian
Problems fixed better and
faster. Fuller information
giving advance warning of other
problems in the pipeline

Figure 4.4

more about how to cope with future problems than under the old bawling-out system; and the organization benefits from problems being identified and tackled at an earlier stage. The vicious circle of suspicion and cover-ups is broken.

The advantages of BMod
I have discussed Rick's problem with Ian at some length because it admirably highlights some of the advantages the BMod approach offers in contrast to other, more traditional approaches.

> Advantage 1   The BMod approach is optimistic rather than pessi-mistic about solving people-problems.

Rick and his colleagues could have been so daunted by the hopelessness of the problem that they might have sat tight and done nothing. It would have been easy to keep their heads down, grin and bear it and wait for Ian to go away. The optimism of the BMod approach encourages people to do *something* rather than shrug their shoulders and accept a bad situation.

> Advantage 2   The BMod approach avoids the problem-solving cul-de-sacs into which the motives, attitudes and feelings route takes you.

Rick can solve the problem with Ian without speculating about Ian's motives or deeper-seated factors to do with his personality make-up.

> Advantage 3   The BMod approach whittles down large, often seemingly impossible problems to size.

Modifying Ian's whole managerial style, be it autocratic or otherwise, would be a horrendous task. It all seems much more manageable once the problem behaviour has been pin-pointed. Modifying Ian from pouncing to helping is still a big task, but spelling things out in behavioural units makes it all possible.

> Advantage 4   The BMod approach encourages people to manage the external environment, which is exactly what they should be doing anyway.

Managing cues and pay-offs requires people to be more thoughtful and less slapdash in their approach, but in essence does not require a manager to do extra things that take him beyond his scope of responsibility.

> Advantage 5   The BMod approach works where other approaches have been tried and found wanting.

In fact, the BMod approach is at its best in circumstances where more traditional approaches have failed to make a satisfactory and permanent impact on the problem.

> Advantage 6   The BMod approach is one that anyone, anywhere in a hierarchy can adopt.

We have just seen that a subordinate (Rick) can use BMod to modify the behaviour of his boss (Ian). It works just as well in any other relationship: manager modifying subordinate, colleague modifying colleague, seller modifying buyer, and so on.

> Advantage 7   The BMod approach modifies observable behaviour and this makes it easy to verify.

Since behaviour is by definition overt, it is a straightforward matter to validate any modification strategy—either one behaviour decreases and the other increases or it does not. Your own observations or those of colleagues will tell you. You need not be in any doubt.

Later, in Chapter 8, I will redress the balance a little by examining the limitations of the BMod approach. We will also look at the ethics of the approach. Is it unacceptably manipulative? What is manipulation anyway? Is it essentially a furtive process or can it be done openly? Is it dangerous? Can it back-fire on you and bring about a worse situation than you started with? Meanwhile, let us return to the two outstanding problems in Chapter 1 and see if we can solve them using the BMod approach.

Overloaded Ted

We shall start, as before, with a list of Ted's disappointments about his director's behaviour. From the description, Ted has four of them:
1. His director loads 'far too much work' on him.
2. He sets deadlines that 'are absurdly tight'.
3. He is reluctant to take any initiative in throwing light on the meaning of the data Ted takes to him.
4. He turns Ted's questions back.
We can use the BMod approach to solve any one of these problems; the question is, which is the major one from Ted's point of view. The real-life Ted reckoned it was the first on our list, with the second closely connected. He admitted that problems three and four were disappointing but not as pressing as the overload problem.

So the behaviour Ted wants to modify in his boss is 'loads too much work on him'. Now we need to look for cues that trigger this behaviour. What is it that happens *before* the director loads work on Ted that appears to trigger it? We do not have to search for long. In the description of the problem on page 4 it says: 'This seems to happen whenever Ted goes to him with a work problem' and later 'at the end of these meetings'. What has happened *before* one of the director's bouts of overloading is that Ted has had one of his sessions where he tried, in vain according to the description, to pick his director's brains on the interpretation of statistical data.

This may now seem obvious to you from the description of the problem, but in real life Ted had not figured this out; it was only when he started to think about a possible cue that it dawned on him that his director did not *always* overload him with work. It did not happen at the end of *every* meeting with him: it did not happen, for example, at progress meetings they had from time to time, nor at meetings initiated by the sales director, nor at meetings they attended together called by other people. It only happened at the end of the meetings Ted requested on the interpretation of statistical data, and it only happened when the director had dodged Ted's questions by turning them back. Ted's analysis provides us with a cue and behaviour as shown in Figure 4.5.

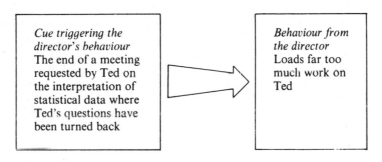

Cue triggering the director's behaviour
The end of a meeting requested by Ted on the interpretation of statistical data where Ted's questions have been turned back

Behaviour from the director
Loads far too much work on Ted

Figure 4.5

Let us turn our attention to the pay-off. What happens *after* the sales director has overloaded Ted that appears to be a satisfactory outcome for him (the sales director)? This is rather more obscure, as pay-offs frequently are, and the temptation to retreat into internal speculations is strong. After all, it could be that the sales director is made to feel inadequate when Ted comes to him with statistical data and a list of open-ended, unanswerable questions; perhaps he does not answer the questions because he is *unable* and deeply resents Ted putting him in this uncomfortable position. He might therefore load work on Ted to redress the balance, to re-establish his superiority, to feel in charge again.

These may or may not be the sales director's conscious or unconscious motives in overloading Ted; we can only speculate since the director's motives are not easily verifiable because they are covert. Instead, let us see if we can find pay-offs by examining the external events that occur after the overloading of Ted. We know from the description that Ted 'moves heaven and earth to get through it all in addition to his "normal" on-going work'. So, on the face of it, a pay-off for the sales director is that he gets more work out of Ted; when overloaded, Ted literally does more than when he is not. Why, then, does the sales director not overload Ted all the time and not just at the end of one of these interpretive sessions? The description does not tell us but in real life we would need to check to see if there was a tie-up here. Ted found there was. When he thought it through, he discovered that the frequency of their interpretive meetings was decreasing—when he first reported to the sales director (some two years ago), they had interpretive-type sessions every couple of weeks; now the meetings were down to four or

43

five a year. So, for whatever reason, a possible pay-off for the sales director is that he avoids interpretive sessions with Ted as well as getting more work out of him!

Figure 4.6 now illustrates the full picture.

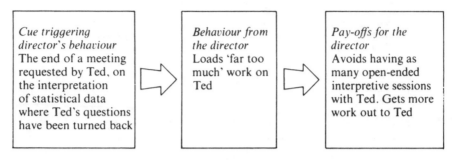

Cue triggering director's behaviour
The end of a meeting requested by Ted, on the interpretation of statistical data where Ted's questions have been turned back

Behaviour from the director
Loads 'far too much' work on Ted

Pay-offs for the director
Avoids having as many open-ended interpretive sessions with Ted. Gets more work out to Ted

Figure 4.6

So how can Ted make any impact on this sequence of events? The first step is for him to be clear about the behaviour he desires. What is it he would rather his director did than conclude the meeting by loading too much work on him? Ted decided that he wanted the director to thank him for an interesting session and ask to be kept informed of future developments. To trigger this rather than the overloading behaviour, Ted had to think of some way to change the existing cue. Suppose he went to the meetings with a list of interpretations rather than a list of open-ended questions? That might succeed in reversing things and winning the sales director's active participation. After all, if Ted, the 'expert', has questions he does not know the answers to, why should he expect his director to fare any better, especially since it appears that he is unable to and fobs off the questions by saying they are Ted's province? Ted must make it a personal rule never to ask an open-ended question requiring interpretation in the meetings; instead, he must concentrate on offering answers or solutions. This will make it more likely that the director will show interest and join Ted in the exploration of alternatives.

So now the changed cue and behaviour are as in Figure 4.7.

That is half the story; the other half brings us back to pay-offs. Ted needs to have a way of encouraging the new behaviour and discouraging the old. The new cue automatically helps to ensure a decrease in open-ended interpretive sessions; that is good because we suspected that one of the director's pay-offs in overloading Ted was that he successfully decreased interpretive sessions. We also noticed that the overloading resulted in the director getting more work out of Ted. So now it is beginning to become clear what Ted needs to do at the pay-off end of the formula.

New cue triggering the director's behaviour
The end of a meeting where different interpretations of statistical data have been explored

New behaviour from the director
Thanks Ted for an interesting session and says he looks forward to hearing about further developments

Figure 4.7

When the director concludes by thanking Ted for an interesting session, etc., Ted must be careful to reward him with *less* open-ended interpretive sessions and with *more* work.

When the director concludes by overloading him, Ted must be careful to ask some open-ended interpretive-type questions and to work less hard on the extra work load. This is not to suggest that Ted becomes awkward and does not do any of the extra work—we know that is 'out of character'. He could, ensure, however, that he did *relatively* less work when overloaded and more work when the director had behaved as Ted wished; Ted could even 'reward' the director by asking if there was anything extra he wanted him to tackle! The chances are the director would be sufficiently surprised not to overload and certainly not to set unrealistically tight deadlines!

In summary, the BMod solution to Ted's problem can be shown in Figure 4.8.

New cue triggering the director's behaviour
The end of a meeting where different interpretations of statistical data have been explored

New behaviour from the sales director
Director thanks Ted for an interesting session and says he looks forward to hearing about further developments

New pay-offs for the sales director
Less open-ended interpretive sessions/questions.
Ted asks 'Is there anything additional you'd like me to tackle?'

Figure 4.8

45

Notice that this solution to the problem was advantageous to both men. Ted was no longer overloaded and got more value out of the meetings with his director. The sales director had sessions with Ted that were more interesting/worth while and Ted is even more willing than usual!

Bert, the supervisor

Let us conclude by seeing how the BMod approach solved the problem with Maureen. If you remember, Bert's disappointments with her are that she does not get through her work quota. More specifically, she takes too long over the coding and categorizing of vouchers. Things come to a head as the deadline approaches: 'Virtually every morning at present there is a mad scramble to get the invoices ready for dispatch by 10.00 hours.'

Let us select 'She takes too long over the coding and categorizing of vouchers' as the problem behaviour and see if we can identify a cue. You will see that we are rather short of specific data; the description on page 5 says: 'He is not sure why she takes too long over the coding and categorizing.' This means that Bert would need to assemble some more data. It need not be anything too elaborate, but he should pin-point when she takes too long more precisely. For example, does she work faster in the morning than in the afternoon? Is there a pattern that would be revealed by an hourly check? Is there a pattern that would be revealed by a daily check? For example, what happens to Maureen's work rate on Tuesdays when the weekly batch arrives?

In the event, Bert decided to keep a closer eye on Maureen for a week to check how many vouchers had been processed at the end of each morning and afternoon. Table 4.1 shows what he found.

This shows that Maureen has a tendency to process fewer vouchers the more there are to do—it is almost as though the sight of piles of unprocessed vouchers slows her down. When they begin to diminish, she speeds up. This can be shown as in Figure 4.9.

What about Maureen's pay-off? The description says: 'Everyone pitches in and lends a hand . . . The vouchers and invoices are always ready by the

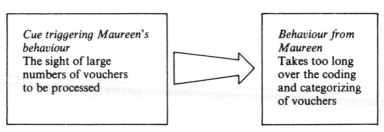

Cue triggering Maureen's behaviour
The sight of large numbers of vouchers to be processed

Behaviour from Maureen
Takes too long over the coding and categorizing of vouchers

Figure 4.9

Table 4.1

Day	Vouchers to be processed				Vouchers actually processed		
	Daily batch	Weekly batch	Total		Daily batch	Weekly batch	Total
Tue	25	* 89 ⎫ † 528 ⎭ 642	642	am pm	— 20	70 30	120
Wed	58	‡ 498	556	am pm	22 24	40 35	121
Thur	55	‡ 423	478	am pm	29 18	45 60	152
Fri	32	‡ 318	350	am pm	13 19	63 55	150
Mon	56	‡ 200	256	am pm	20 25	73 60	178

* Balance of last week's batch.   † New weekly batch.   ‡ Balance left each day.

deadline—it is just that Maureen never gets through the work without eleventh-hour assistance.' So the advantage to Maureen in going slow is that other people pitch in and polish off the outstanding vouchers. It is obviously advantageous to Maureen to keep up her disappointing behaviour. Our cue, behaviour and pay-off can now be shown in Figure 4.10.

Armed with this analysis of the existing situation, let us see how Bert could modify Maureen's behaviour. If we assume that he wanted Maureen to process the vouchers, without assistance, by the deadline, how could he change the cue to trigger this new behaviour?

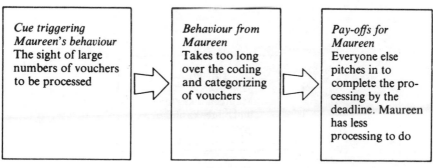

Cue triggering Maureen's behaviour The sight of large numbers of vouchers to be processed

Behaviour from Maureen Takes too long over the coding and categorizing of vouchers

Pay-offs for Maureen Everyone else pitches in to complete the processing by the deadline. Maureen has less processing to do

Figure 4.10

I expect you can see an obvious solution—Bert will have to introduce a new system so that the flow of vouchers through to Maureen is controlled. For example, Bert could control the flow on a daily, half-daily, two-hourly or hourly basis; it depends on what is feasible in the light of all his supervisory duties. In real life, Bert adopted a half-daily basis. His system was simple. First thing on Tuesday afternoon, he divided the freshly arrived weekly batch of vouchers by five, the number of working days available to clear them; this gave him an 'index' of how many weekly vouchers needed to be processed each day. He then adjusted this index up or down depending on the daily batch of vouchers. This arrangement dramatically altered the old cue.

As for the pay-off, Bert agreed with Maureen that she must complete the target on a half-daily basis. If the morning target was not completed, she must finish it before going to lunch, or if the afternoon target had not been reached, before going home. Conversely, if she finished her quota early, she could either go to lunch early/have a longer lunch break, or start the afternoon quota before lunch and go home early when the daily target was reached. All help was withdrawn.

This combination of altered cues and pay-offs did the trick; Maureen achieved her targets, often with time in hand. Figure 4.11 shows the BMod solution to the problem.

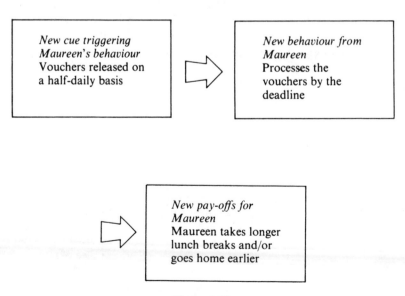

Figure 4.11

Conclusion

In this chapter I have demonstrated how BMod solved three persistent people-problems. In each case:
- The problem behaviour was defined.
- The cues triggering it were identified.
- The pay-offs sustaining it were identified.
- The new behaviour was defined.
- New cues were thought out.
- New pay-offs were arrived at.

The first three steps in this sequence are BMod's way of analysing the existing problem; the latter three are BMod's way of producing a solution. The whole approach depends for its success on the basic tenet that people behave in *reaction* to cues and in *anticipation* of pay-offs.

In subsequent chapters I shall give many more illustrations of people-problems that have been successfully solved using BMod. Meanwhile, having seen the advantages of BMod for solving specific people-problems, let us broaden our perspectives by looking at how people-problems are caused and at how the BMod approach can help improve the management of people.

5. Why people-problems are so prevalent

Now that I have introduced the essence of the BMod approach and demonstrated how it can be used to solve specific people-problems, I want to look at some of its broader implications. In this chapter we will see how the BMod approach throws light on some of the puzzling aspects of people's behaviour in organizations. Why are people-problems so prevalent? Why do people so frequently behave inappropriately? Are people-problems inevitable or can they be prevented? BMod gives some refreshingly new answers to these questions. Many of the answers are hard to accept at first because BMod frequently challenges the assumptions we tend to make about people, and indicates that we should reverse current practice and literally stand it on its head. This theme will be continued in the next chapter when we look at how the BMod framework affects the management of people.

The effect of rewards and punishments

Let us start our broader look at BMod by examining the effect that rewards and punishments (or carrots and sticks) have on people's behaviour in a work setting. Ostensibly every organization, large or small, is structured to get tasks done effectively; in theory this is done by creating a working environment where a balance is struck between encouraging people to do the right things and discouraging them from doing the wrong things. I am going to argue that, in practice, organizations often achieve precisely the opposite. I will illustrate this point with two true stories.

THE CASE OF THE 'HIGH-FLYING' GRADUATES
A large organization recruited graduates as part of an annual management trainee scheme. They spent thousands of pounds each year touring all the universities, interviewing prospective candidates, organizing 'country house'-style selection boards, and finally securing the services of 30 brand-new, eager graduates. The philosophy behind this scheme was to bring new blood into the organization and give them high-flyer status so that the maximum number would reach managerial posts within three years. Accordingly, the selection procedures were consciously biased towards graduates with 'get-up-and-go' charisma (the company's expression). A great deal of store was placed upon their ability to be creative, to tackle problems using lateral thinking, and to display entrepreneurial tendencies. All graduates had to be first- or second-class honours.

The competition to secure such high-calibre graduates was naturally fierce, but the organization was careful to pay them over the odds and this, plus the company's household name, invariably did the trick.

Once recruited, each graduate was put through a long induction programme which took the form of a series of week-long courses punctuated with assignments designed to circulate them around all the key departments in the company. Much of the time was spent painstakingly telling the graduates about the history of the organization and instructing them in its formal structures, policies and procedures (of which there were many). Typically, the graduates found this an awful bore and enormously pedestrian in contrast to their recent university experiences. The instructors who took the courses were all 'old hands' who knew the organization's customs and practices inside out. Not surprisingly, the instructors resented the graduates' 'high-flyer' status and showed it in a host of small but significant ways; they were sticklers for punctuality, for example, and were fond of talking down to the graduates at every opportunity. At first the graduates took this in good humour, but eventually formed a more jaundiced view of their instructors.

The series of attachments to different departments around the organization exacerbated the situation. Each posting was for a period of six weeks, which was too short to get them stuck into anything worth while and too long for a superficial exploratory visit. Departmental supervisors made it pretty clear to the graduates that they were a 'nuisance' and rarely gave them worth while tasks to tackle. Most of the time, graduates on attachment hung around grossly underemployed, killing time, looking and feeling 'spare'. Their boredom was intense.

Occasionally, as part of the induction, the graduates were given a project to tackle. The majority of the projects had been presented to their predecessors and were coming round for the second or third time. The graduates had to produce a project report and present it to a panel of senior managers drawn from different parts of the organization. The usual pattern which emerged at these sessions was for the panel to test the graduates' ideas to destruction; the senior managers did this by pointing out how naïve and impractical the graduates' suggestions were, and frequently 'pulled rank' by quoting past precedents. The whole process was rather undignified and the senior managers invariably 'won' (in the sense that they scored points over the graduates).

It will not surprise you to hear that senior management were unimpressed with the graduates' performance; there were constant debates among them about the wisdom of recruiting graduates at all. They complained that modern universities were turning out graduates who were lacking in originality, not prepared to work their way up from the bottom, too flippant and disruptive to the non-graduate employees, and disloyal (60 per cent of the intake left before the three years were up); these shortcomings were firmly placed at the door

51

of the educational system. It never occurred to management that they might have any responsibility for the graduates' disappointing behaviour.

This true story illustrates just how easy it is for managers actively to discourage the very behaviours they claim to require. The induction process was unwittingly structured to knock the stuffing out of the graduates and turn those that survived into obedient zombies. Given this state of affairs, it was entirely predictable that the best (i.e., the most 'creative', 'charismatic', etc.) graduates would get up and go; only the cautious and less creative were likely to remain.

The stated objective of having a graduate intake scheme (namely to attract high flyers who would reach managerial posts within three years) was, therefore, not achieved. An understanding of BMod principles could have prevented this problem and saved a great deal of time and money.

THE CASE OF THE DEPARTMENTAL MANAGER WHO VOLUNTEERED
TO CUT HIS BUDGET

In another company a senior manager, with three departmental managers reporting to him, had his budget cut by the managing director. The cuts were substantial and could not be met by simply manipulating the figures or making fringe adjustments here and there. The senior manager was loath to announce arbitrary, across-the-board cuts that were identical for each department because some budgeted projects were of higher priority than others. He decided to invite all three departmental managers to a meeting with him so that cut-back areas and projects could be mutually agreed.

Prior to the meeting he briefed each departmental manager, putting them fully in the picture about the overall size of the cut-back and asking them to prepare for the meeting by putting projects in priority order vis-à-vis the overall business objectives.

At the meeting he was alarmed to discover that all three departmental managers took up entrenched defensive positions and refused to volunteer cuts in the way he had hoped for; this was disappointing because his relationship with the three managers had always been harmonious and cooperative. Eventually, after a long period of deadlock, one of the departmental managers volunteered to cut back on a project in his department. Instead of triggering similar offers from the other two departmental managers, the reverse happened; remaining projects in the volunteering manager's department came under even more stringent scrutiny until eventually he finished up having sacrificed more than anyone else.

After the meeting the volunteering manager remarked that he had learned his lesson: 'I'll never volunteer anything again if this is where it gets me.'

It is often said that busy people (i.e., people who tend to volunteer for things) are the best people to have around when there are extra jobs to be done. Once they cotton on to the fact that they are being exploited, however, people who were initially willing become a great deal less so. To think I was once puzzled by an army sergeant-major who used to call for volunteers and then give the nasty jobs to people who did not put up their hands—he knew how to get people to volunteer!

BMod is a continual reminder that people behave the way they do in reaction to, and in anticipation of, external events in their working environment. Whenever we are puzzled or disappointed about people's behaviour, BMod prompts us to ask three revealing questions:
1. Are the existing cues triggering the inappropriate behaviour?
2. Are the existing pay-offs:
  (a) encouraging the inappropriate behaviour?
  (b) discouraging the appropriate behaviour?
  (c) both (a) and (b)?
3. Are both cues and pay-offs wrong?
The graduate induction scheme is an excellent example of both cues and pay-offs being all to pot. The senior managers, departmental supervisors and instructors were completely oblivious to the part they had played in bringing about the very behaviours they complained about; they simply did not see the connection between their own behaviour and that of the graduates. As far as they were concerned, either the graduates themselves were to blame or the 'educational system'.

The case of the volunteering manager shows how readily people are penalized even when they behave appropriately. The senior manager failed to see the topsy-turvy connection between volunteering and sacrificing more than those who did not volunteer. In effect he was encouraging his managers *not* to volunteer, and yet we can readily imagine him bemoaning the fact that people were so uncooperative.

BMod helps us to see that the working environment is a crucial contributor to how people behave. If people are doing the 'wrong' things, then it is likely that the environment has brought this about. People-problems are prevalent because the influence of the working environment goes largely unheeded; in other words, people-problems are literally *created* when insufficient attention is paid to the effect that cues and pay-offs have on behaviour.

Let us look at another example that throws light on why many meetings are unproductive.

THE UNPRODUCTIVE MEETING
Imagine you are due to attend an important meeting and that a number of papers have been circulated in advance as required reading in preparation for the meeting. You dutifully find time to study the papers, think about the problems they pose and generally get yourself thoroughly prepared; you also get to the meeting on time, taking all the relevant papers with you. So far so good.

At the meeting a number of things happen that inconvenience you. For a start, some key participants are not there on time; you and others who are on time hang around waiting. (Lesson 1 so far as you are concerned: there is no point in arriving at meetings punctually.) After a while the meeting gets under way; the most senior manager present says he has not had time to read all the bumph and could the relevant authors please summarize their submissions for the meeting. A number of other participants readily support this request. Three inadequate, tedious and, for you, quite unnecessary oral summaries ensue. Those who have not prepared by reading the papers are now being 'rewarded' for not doing so; those who have prepared are being 'punished' by the sheer boredom of unnecessarily and inadequately going over old ground. (Lesson 2: there is no point in preparing for meetings.) After the oral submissions, the chairman invites discussion. You are alarmed to notice that the unprepared participants proceed to hog the discussion.

Instead of coming up with alternative ideas on what should be done to solve the problems, the discussion is almost exclusively devoted to questions of clarification and information. The unprepared are using the discussion to fill in the remaining gaps in their understanding that resulted from not reading the papers in advance. (Lesson 2 is reinforced: there is no point in preparing for meetings.) Eventually you have had enough and decide to put forward an idea you have for solving one of the problems. Immediately after you have advanced your idea, certain members of the meeting turn on you and disagree with it; in your view, their objections are based upon misconceptions about the nature of the problem. You do your best to explain the merits of your idea, but the opposition is too strong and eventually you think 'What the hell' and fall silent. (Lesson 3: it is not worth sticking out your neck and proposing an idea.)

After further wrangling, the meeting finishes inconclusively with the unprepared participants having the audacity to call for an additional written report to be produced and circulated before the next meeting! (Lesson 4: meetings are a waste of time.)

How could the use of BMod have solved this problem? Basically, by making sure that appropriate behaviours were duly rewarded and that inappropriate behaviours were not:

- As a punctual person you should have been 'rewarded' by the meeting starting bang on time instead of being 'punished' by having to hang around for latecomers.
- As a prepared person you should have been 'rewarded' with an informed discussion based on the written papers instead of being 'punished' by having to listen to a tedious reiteration of the ground already covered more adequately in the papers.
- As a person who produced ideas you should have been 'rewarded' by having your ideas supported or developed, or at least subjected to *informed*

scrutiny, instead of being 'punished' by the ignorant demolition of your ideas.

The conscious application of BMod would transform this, and no doubt many other meetings by actively encouraging desirable behaviours and discouraging undesirable ones. A final example follows.

WHY MANAGERS ARE SO OFTEN RELUCTANT TO MANAGE

One of the most widespread criticisms levelled against management at all levels is that they spend too much time tackling tasks that they should be getting other people to do. The result is that managers frequently spend too high a proportion of time 'doing' and not enough managing. Examples of this are readily apparent; here are just four:

- Managers attending to detail instead of dealing with larger issues and 'managing by exception'.
- Managers failing to delegate because, having had experience in the past, they are certain they can do the job better themselves.
- Managers getting caught in the vicious circle of day-to-day fire-fighting and short-term activities instead of planning in advance.
- Managers preferring to do tangible tasks and avoiding the more thinking activities of planning and organizing.

Of course, circumstances vary from organization to organization, but in general the reason why so many managers are reluctant to manage and would rather 'do' is plain to see; they like it because they get more pay-offs for their behaviour when they operate than they do when they manage. When were you last positively 'rewarded' for planning as opposed to saving the day by solving some crisis or other? Can you recall being frequently 'rewarded' for delegating a task that you would have done well and would dearly have loved to tackle yourself? The truth is that most of the classical managerial activities such as planning, organizing, leading and controlling are inherently more difficult and/or less rewarding than the alternative, that temptingly presents itself each day, of doing it yourself.

Rewarding means, not end results

What needs to be done to make managing an attractive proposition? BMod provides the answer that, in principle, ways need to be found to 'reward' means, not just ends. At present, managers tend to be judged purely by the results they achieve with little regard to how they got there. However important though results are, the day-in, day-out process of managing is primarily about employing the right means to maximize the chances of securing the end results. So managers should be positively rewarded for:

- Avoiding detail and sticking to larger issues.
- Managing by exception.

- Delegating responsibility and commensurate authority (particularly when the task to be done is one the manager is 'expert' at).
- Predetermining courses of action by objective setting and planning.

Clearly, it is not as easy to think of how to reward managers for indulging in these on-going activities as opposed to the more tangible 'doing' activities and the achievement of end results; until this is done, however, it is predictable that managers will continue to be busy doing the wrong things. In the next chapter I shall be returning to the issue of what, in BMod terms, constitutes a 'reward', but for the time being let me give some examples of how on-going managerial activities could be positively encouraged:

1. Whenever a manager says something like 'I don't know the answer to that at present because I've delegated it to Joe and he isn't due to report back until Friday', his boss should say 'Fine. I leave it to you. Don't bother to let me know unless there is some snag you think I can help with.'

2. Pay managers a monthly bonus for having up-to-date objectives and plans:
   - that are actively referred to;
   - that are modified in the light of new data;
   - that meet laid-down specificity/precision standards.

3. Do one or more of the following things for managers who avoid getting bogged down in detail, manage by exception, delegate effectively and have objectives and plans:
   - Give them more of something they enjoy doing.
   - Give them extra days off.
   - Give them a sabbatical period to study a subject of their choice at a university of their choice.
   - Involve them in a genuinely vital project which utilizes their management skills to the full.
   - Get them to show other managers how to develop similar skills.

Conclusion

There are many more examples illustrating how topsy-turvy the rewards and punishments, or carrots and sticks, are in most organizational settings. To round off this chapter, Table 5.1 provides a list of desirable behaviours that tend to go unrewarded and undesirable behaviours that tend, unwittingly, to be rewarded.

This list reminds us that people's behaviour is constantly being influenced by the environment and that people are frequently encouraged to do the very things we wish they would not do! When the BMod approach is used as a conscious, systematic and consistent framework, the sort of problems we have discussed in this chapter can be prevented or corrected.

In this chapter I have argued that many of our people-problems are of our own creation and that we are likely to continue to create them while we pay insufficient attention to cues and pay-offs. In the next chapter I shall examine how the conscious application of BMod improves the management of people and reduces people-problems.

Table 5.1

Encouraged Behaviour	*Discouraged Behaviour*
Spend all the budget allocation before the year end	Cut costs/save money
Play it safe	Take a calculated risk
Secure short-term gains	Take a longer-term view
Do not rock the boat	Criticize the system and push for improvements
Play things by ear	Set clear, realistic and yet challenging objectives
Take immediate remedial action. Do what has been done before	Think through a problem before implementing the best solution
Cover up mistakes and never admit to problems or shortcomings	Declare problems/mistakes/shortcomings
Never ask for help—it is an admission of weakness	Ask for help/advice
Seek approval—claim popular decisions as your own and blame unpopular ones on someone else	Make and implement unpopular decisions
Compete with other departments. Be secretive—play things close to your chest	Cooperate with other departments. Be open
Keep busy	Think
Repeat same mistakes over and over again. Do not review experience—no one will notice	Learn from experience
Stick to the tried and true	Experiment with a new approach
Criticize other people's ideas	Accept and develop other people's ideas
Keep all the best/prestige jobs for yourself. Only delegate routine	Develop subordinates
Stick to the facts all the time	Think laterally by suspending judgement and thinking wild
Be earnest, look serious	Do not take yourself too seriously

6. *The new approach and the management of people*

In the last chapter we saw how people-problems arise when BMod is not used. In this chapter I am going to show you how consciously to apply BMod to the management of people. Besides being an excellent way of solving specific people-problems, the BMod approach spawns many additional guidelines for the practising manager. In this chapter I am going to highlight five of these guidelines, namely:
1. It is better to reward the 'right' behaviours than to punish the wrong ones.
2. Short-term pay-offs are more effective than long-term ones.
3. Managers are responsible for performance, not for satisfying people's needs.
4. Managers should manage individuals, not people *en masse*.
5. BMod can enhance performance improvement activities, like coaching and appraising.

It is better to reward the 'right' behaviours than to punish the wrong ones

I expect you have already noticed that, in all the solutions to people-problems we have looked at so far, I have been at pains to emphasize the positive and to have possible sanctions very much in reserve. The very essence of pay-offs is that they are welcomed by the *recipient* as being 'nice' or rewarding. To illustrate this, let me hark back for a moment to the solutions to people-problems I have already cited:
– The husband with the nagging wife was careful to *reward* her when she first asked him to fix something by immediately committing himself to a date 10 days from the time of asking (a great deal earlier than under the old nagging system). It was only when his wife slipped into nagging that sanctions were reluctantly imposed and the fixing date was postponed.
– The personnel manager with the 'stroppy' shop steward was careful to grant more concessions when the shop steward made *reasonable* demands and only withheld concessions when the shop steward took an unreasonable posture.
– Ron had a problem with his boss who too frequently circumvented him. The solution was for Ron to encourage increased consultation by agreeing with his boss when he consulted Ron and, when he *had* to disagree (on matters of principle, for example), to find more agreeable ways of doing so.
– Rick was anxious to stop Ian's tendency to 'pounce' and sort out problems himself. His solution was, first and foremost, to reward Ian by ensuring

that problems were fixed better and faster when he 'helped', and only as a second priority to thwart him when he pounced.

- Ted wanted to stop his director loading so much work on him. He brought this about by rewarding the director with less inconvenient, open-ended interpretive sessions and by working relatively harder when the director had behaved as he wished. The obvious sanction of doing less work was only used if his director persisted in overloading him.
- Bert wanted to increase Maureen's productivity in processing vouchers. He did this by rewarding her with longer lunch breaks and letting her home earlier. He only applied sanctions reluctantly when she failed to get through her half-day quota of vouchers.

Notice how, in every case, positive, rewarding pay-offs followed hard on the heels of the desired behaviour. The other side of the coin, sanctions to punish the undesirable behaviour, are used only as a last resort and always in stark contrast to the positive aspects of the solution. It is as though the negative is used to highlight and enhance the positive.

This emphasis on rewarding the right behaviour is quite unlike the way behaviour is normally regulated at work; in most work settings, this is done on more of a punitive basis by punishing, or threatening to punish, undesirable behaviours. Consider the following everyday occurrences and you will agree that life is more often punishing than rewarding:

1. You get up earlier than usual in order to get to work in time for an important meeting. You get caught in a traffic jam and arrive late.
2. Your usual parking area is full and you have to cruise around to find another slot. Reversing too hurriedly into too tight a space, you dent a front wing on a concrete bollard.
3. Your secretary has filed the papers you need for the meeting and had deliberately left out overnight. She promises to extricate them from the files and bring them along to you at the meeting. In the event, she fails to bring a rather important appendix that you have done some vital calculations on.
4. The chairman of the meeting makes sarcastic remarks about your being late.
5. The meeting goes badly, you fail to make your point and the decision goes against you.
6. You get back to your office to find a whole pile of urgent messages waiting for you. You start to clear them but are soon thwarted because certain key people you need to contact are not available until later.
7. A customer telephones you with a complaint and threatens to cancel his order and place it with the competition.
8. You go to see your boss in order to get some reaction from him over an important report you have submitted in draft. The session is abortive because:

(a) he has not read it all yet.
(b) the bit he has read he does not agree with and wants substantially altering.
(c) he returns your latest expenses form unsigned because of some petty irregularity.
(d) he breaks the bad news that certain jobs in your department have not been regraded as you hoped, and that a head-count freeze has just been announced which will prevent you from recruiting.

9. You get back to your office to find electricians removing ceiling panels in order to install a new heat-detector system. Furthermore, a red sticker has been put on your telephone saying 'before noon's too soon', with a reminder about a new rule forbidding trunk calls in the morning.

10. Just as you have resettled and got down to work again, security telephone to ask you to move your car because it is blocking deliveries to the canteen.

Need I go on? The ratio of punishments to rewards means that most behaviour at work is geared to avoiding unpleasant consequences rather than positively striving to secure pay-offs. Naturally, people do not perform as well as they might when they are busy looking over their shoulders in anticipation of the next brickbat. I shall be looking at some of the research evidence that supports this and related matters in the next chapter. The more conscious use of BMod by practising managers would redress this imbalance by building in positive pay-offs for desirable behaviour rather than relying almost exclusively on sanctions to prevent undesirable behaviour.

Short-term pay-offs are more effective than long-term ones

It is often said that man is a purposeful animal, and BMod endorses this by showing how people behave in anticipation of future consequences, either to achieve pay-offs or to avoid sanctions. There is, however, a very important BMod principle that reminds us that people's purposes are often only short term. Empirical evidence shows that, to be effective, pay-offs and sanctions should happen hard on the heels of the behaviour in question. As we have seen, a pay-off (or sanction) has to be associated with the occurrence of a certain behaviour if it is to have any effect; under these conditions, pay-offs are likely to increase the frequency of the behaviour and sanctions are likely to decrease it. Clearly, if the gap in time between the behaviour and its consequence is too wide (with many intervening events), the two events are not likely to be linked. For example, suppose someone does a particularly commendable piece of work and six months later I reward them for it with a bonus of some kind; in these circumstances the bonus is most unlikely to encourage a repetition of the high level of performance. The things that happened closer in time to the production of the work are far more likely to act as encouragers or discouragers.

In BMod parlance this is known as the 'contingency concept'. When a consequence (pay-off or sanction) is applied contingently, it means that it:
- is conditional upon the occurrence of the behaviour in question.
- follows the occurrence of the behaviour quickly enough for the association, or link, to be apparent.

If you apply the contingency concept to many of the events at work, you will discover that rewards and punishments are frequently presented in a non-contingent way—either they are haphazard rather than conditional and/or do not happen quickly enough. This explains why people sometimes behave in apparently self-defeating or irrational ways and forgo rewards.

Money is a controversial example of a reward that rarely meets the contingency criteria. Certainly, if you are on a monthly salary, the gap between working and receiving the cheque is too long. Furthermore, most salaried employees have discovered that their performance during the month makes no difference one way or the other to the monthly pay cheque; it is virtually automatic and not conditional upon performance in any way. Of course there are administrative problems, but if money was to be made a genuine pay-off that encouraged desired performance, we would all be on a daily piece-rate system. We would also physically receive actual money or goods rather than a distant (invisible) bank transfer.

This helps to explain why researches into what motivates people to work have tended to put money lower down the league table than people can usually credit. In my own case, I am the first to admit that the anticipation of money gets me to turn up but has little impact on the standard of my performance when I am there; whether I merely go through the motions or pull out all the stops is dependent upon other, more immediate factors. For example, if people react to what I have to offer in an interested, enthusiastic way, I am greatly encouraged and work far harder than if the reaction is deadpan and indifferent. Salary administration has effectively killed money as a motivator in itself by ensuring that it is rarely contingent upon performance.

The contingency concept throws light on other, apparently puzzling aspects of people's behaviour. Why, for example, do people strike for more pay when studies reveal that, depending on the length of the strike and the size of the settlement, strikers frequently have to work for a year or more to make up the earnings they lost during the strike? At first sight it simply does not make sense. BMod helps us to see that there must be short-term pay-offs that sustain striking behaviour, otherwise it would not happen; it may be the break from routine, the drama of picket duty, the camaraderie, or the lavish attention from the media or even the government. If strikers had no short-term pay-offs, they would stop striking and find an alternative behaviour that was more satisfactory. So how can strikes be prevented? Appeals for restraint based on the threat of dire consequences in the longer term (like fewer jobs, more redundancies, higher inflation, etc.) are clearly inadequate because they fail to take account of the contingency concept. If it is true that strikes succeed in giving people short-term pay-offs, we need to ensure that people get *more* of what they lack (not necessarily *everything* they lack) when they are not striking than they do when they are. This strategy would be a complete reversal of the current state of affairs, when we seem to contrive to ensure that people's 'lacks' increase when they are working normally and decrease as a consequence of striking behaviour.

There are many less dramatic examples of the application of the contingency concept: not praising people at the time but saving it up for a six-monthly or, even worse, an annual appraisal session; not rebuking people at the time but turning a blind eye to a number of 'offences' until they have accumulated over a period and can no longer be ignored; giving someone extra time off because the sun is shining and you are in a good mood. Many times each day a manager is unthinkingly using rewards and punishments in an inconsistent, non-contingent way. The lesson is to identify key behaviours —those you want to increase or decrease—and use short-term pay-offs and sanctions on a here-and-now basis.

Managers are responsible for performance, not for satisfying people's needs

One of the questions most often debated by managers in one form or another is how best to motivate people. This issue seems all the more pressing in today's conditions where managers bemoan the fact that their authority is being steadily eroded; government legislation in employment practices is blamed for diminishing the old hire-and-fire, do-as-I-tell-you-or-else tactics. Now managers have to take account of discrimination and unfair dismissal. Furthermore, as union membership grows, managers claim that the power of the unions increasingly cramps their style; they have to anticipate how the unions will react and concentrate on winning consent before they act. Also, managers have to cope with people who, by and large, have more sophisticated expectations about work itself. Managers have to develop the considerable skills involved in behaving participatively. In these circumstances, with their apparent room for manoeuvre shrinking, managers are puzzled about how to motivate people.

Unfortunately, the answer has been unnecessarily complicated by the assumption that motivation is some sort of internal state or need. Most popular theories of motivation postulate the existence of certain psychological needs, such as the need for safety, esteem and self-actualization. However, no evidence for the existence of any internal motivational state or need has ever been presented that cannot be explained more simply. Take, for example, the idea that needs are arranged in a hierarchy where lower, physiological needs have to be satisfied before higher, psychological ones come into play. Certainly, research substantiates the fact that, if someone is simultaneously deprived of, say, food and love, their behaviour will be directed towards securing food rather than love; it is quite unnecessary, however, to imagine that the explanation for this is anything to do with 'needs'. A more straightforward explanation is that certain external conditions (no food) resulted in observable behaviour (searching for food). The postulation of a need not only introduces academic complications but also leads managers to attempt to solve people-problems less effectively than they might.

The BMod view is simply that people behave in order to obtain what they lack. If they are deprived of food and warmth, it is predictable that they will behave in order to regain them. Conversely, people will not behave in order to obtain what they already have; if someone is not in danger, for example, they will not perform at high levels to obtain safety. So, rather than worry about which factors are motivators and which are hygiene, which needs are satisfied and which are not, the manager needs to ask a simpler, more direct question: for what pay-off will this person work? The answer properly directs the manager's attention to how to arrange the working environment through cues and pay-offs to get the desired reaction. In this way, BMod reminds us that managers are responsible for performance, not for satisfying needs.

Managers should manage individuals, not people *en masse*

Most managers readily acknowledge that people are unique and have individual characteristics which need to be heeded when handling them: some people can be harrassed with good effect, while others need to be handled with kid gloves; some respond well to pressure, others badly; some respond well to incentives, others seem unmoved, and so on. In *practice*, however, most strategies for handling people in organizations are not individually tailored. Certainly, in large organizations with centralized/corporate personnel policies, practices for handling people are likely to be on an across-the-board basis; in effect, rewards and punishments are decided centrally with Mr Average in mind. The argument in favour of regulating personnel practices in this way is two pronged.

Firstly, it is assumed that, in order to be fair to people working in the same organization, they must be treated equally. Upon closer examination, this apparently laudible assumption turns out to be more convenient to the smooth administration of the organization than to individuals within it. Inequitable treatment in one part of the company creates precedents which have repercussions in other parts.

Secondly, it is argued that busy line managers need guidance in such complex matters as how to handle people. Put less flatteringly, this is in effect arguing that managers cannot be trusted to manage people and need to be controlled from the centre to prevent them doing short-sighted expedient things without regard for longer-term repercussions.

Now, of course, there is some truth in both these arguments. If each individual departmental manager within the same organization was given *carte blanche* to hire and fire and reward and punish his people, there would be more chaos than if things were regulated from the top or from the centre. However, BMod principles would certainly argue for the decentralization of practices for handling people, with more responsibility and authority being pushed down to the individual unit manager. Why? In all the people-problems we have looked at so far, the application of BMod involved looking carefully at how the individual was behaving and in what circumstances. It is clear that, given the 'same' conditions, people react differently. This is because, by the time people have finished processing the information they take in about a situation they are in, it is not the 'same' any more; it is a proven fact that no two people see events, things or people in precisely the same way. It is, therefore, inevitable that people will not react to rewards and punishments in the same way. You might imagine, for example, that you are rewarding someone by publicly praising them. In truth, the praised person may be cringing with embarrassment. Similarly, you might imagine that you are punishing someone by dressing them down in front of their colleagues. In truth, they might be revelling in the attention.

In applying BMod we must be careful not to *assume* that something is rewarding or punishing. What matters is how it functions or, in other words, the effect it actually has on behaviour. Quite simply, if you find that a pay-off successfully increases the occurrence of the behaviour you want, then it is rewarding to the person. If, on the other hand, you find that it decreases the behaviour in question or makes no discernible difference one way or the other, then it is not functioning as a reward, no matter how confident you were that it would. So, strictly speaking, a pay-off should only be referred to as such in BMod when it has been found to encourage successfully the desired behaviour. Until then, it is only a *potential* pay-off.

This distinction may seem rather hair-splitting, but in practice it has far-reaching implications. It means that each individual's behaviour is triggered by different cues (not necessarily unique, since others may be cued by the same events) and reinforced by different pay-offs (again, not necessarily unique). It therefore follows that cues and pay-offs cannot be administered at a distance; this must be left to the manager on the spot. Only he is in a position to know what combinations of cues and pay-offs work for the individuals who report to him.

Of course, within the same organization there must be some agreed boundaries, but these should not be so restricting as to effectively prevent the manager from managing his people through the appropriate use of cues and pay-offs.

BMod can enhance performance improvement activities, like coaching and appraising

When introducing the BMod approach in earlier chapters, I have pointed out that it does not need to be a clandestine process—far from it, for in many instances the business of identifying cues and pay-offs and putting together a feasible modification strategy is actually enhanced by tackling it in the open with the person.

If you find this hard to imagine, then I quite understand! BMod tends to strike people, initially at any rate, as a rather cold-blooded, manipulative process that could only work on a furtive basis. I shall take this up again in Chapter 8 when examining limitations and ethics. Meanwhile, let me show you how the BMod approach could be incorporated in an on-the-job coaching or appraising session between a manager and subordinate.

The parallels between coaching, appraising and BMod are obvious enough; they are all aimed at helping someone to improve performance in their current job. They result in a feasible action plan involving both manager and subordinate, and they all break down into two broad phases: identifying the aspects of performance that need improvement, and deciding what can be done to bring about the desired improvements.

We will now look at a dialogue between a subordinate and manager where the manager is *consciously* adopting a BMod approach; assume that the manager has never formally or informally broached the subject of BMod with the subordinate. First, however, is a brief description of the situation prior to the discussion.

Geoff is an area sales manager with 12 salesmen reporting to him. One of them, Harry, has been a sales representative with the company for 12 years. Prior to this, he was a sales engineer within the same company and was, in fact, 'demoted' in terms of position when he became a sales representative because of large-scale organizational changes. Harry is now approaching 60 years of age, he is technically sound, his product knowledge is first class, and he has built up excellent relationships with the customers in his patch.

All in all, he performs extremely well in relation to his job specification—except for one aspect. The problem is that his monthly written reports are far too long, are full of trivia, and what facts there are get mixed up with what Geoff calls 'guff'; it takes Geoff ages to extract the data he needs when compiling his own report covering the whole area.

The monthly reporting system is well established and is a vital upward communication process. In particular, reports are supposed to contain information that salesmen have gathered in conversation with their customers about complaints, needs, order patterns and the activities of the competition (the company operates in a highly competitive market).

65

Geoff decides to have a coaching session with Harry in a bid to improve his monthly reports.

There now follows enough of the dialogue between the two men to show you how Geoff is able to use BMod as a framework for the discussion. I will put notes in the margin to flag the parts that are especially under the influence of BMod. Imagine that the preliminaries are over . . .

GEOFF: Fine, Harry. Now let's come back to this business we touched on earlier about the problem I have extracting the data I need from your monthly reports. Have you got any ideas on how we could solve this?

HARRY: Well, you could give me a list of the items you particularly need and I could include them in a summary.

GEOFF: That would certainly help. I don't want to overload you, however. If anything, I'd like to streamline your monthly report so that it's shorter rather than adding summaries that make it longer. Harry, looking back over your last few reports, I notice that they have varied in length and I remember that sometimes it was easy for me to extract the data I needed and at other times I found it difficult. Here are some examples. Look, it's rather interesting! In September your report was 19 pages long, whereas the next month it was only 8 pages long. In November it was only 9 pages, but in December it was back up to 15. Have you any idea why it varies so much from month to month?

Geoff is searching for a cue

HARRY: I must admit I've never thought about it. I just bung everything down and don't take much notice of the overall length. Presumably it varies in relation to how busy the month has been. You know how much there is to report on customer complaints, for example, or on what the competition has been up to. Take the time when the opposition launched that sales drive back in—was it September or October? October, I think. Well, there was obviously much more to report then.

Harry is suggesting a possible cue

GEOFF: But the October report was one of the shorter ones, Harry.

But it does not check out!

HARRY: Oh, yes, that's true. That's funny . . .

GEOFF: Let's look through the September and October reports to see if they give us a clue.

Geoff is suggesting a bit of on-the-spot research in the hope of identifying the cue

66

Both men spend some time exploring different ideas on what has happened during the month that seems to trigger a long, as opposed to a short, report. Eventually something emerges . . .

GEOFF: I notice that in September I didn't get to visit you, Harry. If you remember, I took a late holiday and couldn't get round to the whole area. In October I visited you, well at least a couple of times. Look, you refer to them here in your report.

Geoff is suggesting a possible cue

HARRY: So you're saying that I might produce longer reports when you don't visit me during the month? That figures, doesn't it? I'd have to include more in the report if I hadn't seen you and had a chat. Does that explain the November and December reports? November was short and December long. Now how many visits did you pay in November? Here we are—four, once a week throughout the month. And in December—once, but of course that's a short month with Christmas and all.

Harry is testing the feasibility of the cue

GEOFF: So it looks as if there *is* a link. You tend to submit long reports in months when I haven't got out to see you much, and shorter ones when I have. Does that make sense?

Geoff is summarizing the cue

HARRY: Yes. Must admit, it had never occurred to me but it stands to reason. Obviously, when I get to talk to you, I can explain things then and need to say less in the written report.

GEOFF: OK. Let's hold that as a thought for a moment. We'll think of what we can do about it in the way of actions in a minute. Now let's see what happens after you have submitted a long report. Do I react differently or something?

Geoff is suggesting they look for a pay-off

HARRY: Do you react differently? Well yes, I'd say so. You probably 'phone me with questions if it's a long report, whereas you don't need to if it's a short one!

Harry is stumbling on a possible pay-off

GEOFF: Well, let's assume that's true for a moment. The point is, what effect does it have on you when I 'phone with lots of supplementary questions?

Geoff is pushing Harry's pay-off ideas farther

HARRY: Oh, I much prefer you to 'phone me than not. I don't expect you can remember just how isolated you feel out there; sometimes it's as though you're working for the customers rather than for the company. I know that sounds daft, but it's true. Sometimes I have to pinch myself to remember what company I work for.

GEOFF: I see. So you're saying that, when you submit a long report, I contact you more than when it's a short one? Fascinating. It had never dawned on me, I must say.

Geoff is summarizing the pay-off

67

HARRY: Well, don't imagine I had realized it quite so clearly, because I hadn't. I don't want you to think it was deliberate or anything like that, it's just that I like to keep in touch. I like it when the company contacts me.

GEOFF: Yes, I can understand that. Let's just summarize, then. We've discovered that you tend to submit long monthly reports when I haven't been out to see you as much as usual during the month, and that after getting a long one I tend to contact you more frequently in the subsequent month. Is that it?

Geoff is summarizing the cue and the pay-off for long reports from Harry

HARRY: Yes, it sounds simple put like that. I'd never have thought of it in a million years.

GEOFF: Nor I. Now let's see what to do about it. Can we assume that it is better from both our points of view for you to submit short reports rather than long ones?

Geoff is moving on to think of a modification strategy. He starts by checking that the desired behaviour is mutually beneficial

HARRY: Well, of course, I'd rather do that. It's less of a hassle for me, no question about it.

GEOFF: And it would be easier for me to extract the information I need for the area reports. So we're agreed on that. Now it's obvious that I need to contact you more often during the month both before and after getting your report. I've got it! Suppose I agree to visit you at least once a fortnight throughout the year, come what may? Often I'll do better than that, but I want to commit myself to a realistic target. Would that help, do you think?

Geoff is suggesting a changed cue

HARRY: Yes, I'm sure it would. Then I can discuss the longer-winded bits of news and leave them out of the report altogether. Also, I could make it routine to 'phone you at the end of the month before I write my report to get some of the stuff off my chest on the 'phone rather than putting it all in the report. Would you mind that?

Harry is developing Geoff's suggestion for a changed cue

GEOFF: Good idea, but I'd rather do it the other way round. I'll 'phone you on the last Wednesday in every month. How's that?

Geoff is developing Harry's development

HARRY: Absolutely fine. This will make a lot of difference.

GEOFF: So that's what I'm going to do before you write your report. Let's just think for a moment about what I need to do after I've received it. It looks as though, if it's short, I should 'phone you and, if it's long, I shouldn't! Do you see what I mean? That would reverse the way things happen at present.

Geoff is suggesting a changed pay-off

HARRY: I see. You're wanting to fix it so that I am contacted more rather than less when I write short reports? Yes, that's clever. I can see that.

GEOFF: Well, let's try it for a trial period and see what happens.

The two men conclude their conversation by agreeing a trial period, re-capping their plan and looking over a sample of a 'good' monthly report as a reminder of the approved 'house style'.

I contend that, without considerable aid from the BMod approach, Geoff would not have been able to steer the conversation with Harry so successfully. It would probably have been a more pedestrian affair with Geoff solemnly going over the approved 'house style' for monthly reports, and with Harry apparently acquiescing. If it had gone along these lines, I doubt that it would have had anything other than a very temporary effect on Harry's monthly reports. The keys to the mystery, namely the cues and pay-offs surrounding long and short reports, would not have been discovered and Harry's verbose reports would have continued to inconvenience Geoff.

The advantages of using BMod as the framework for coaching or appraisal discussions are considerable. BMod helps to ensure that manager and subordinate:

get down to specifics rather than communicating on too 'lofty' a plain.
- stick to examining external conditions surrounding the behaviour rather than unnecessarily complicating the issue.
- produce a specific action plan that is feasible and stands a high probability of being successful.
- both join in a non-threatening exploration of the problem rather than the manager haranguing the subordinate or vice versa! Notice that, in the Geoff–Harry discussion, it was Harry, the subordinate, who identified the pay-off.

Conclusion

In this chapter I have tried to demonstrate the significance of the BMod approach when it comes to managing people. The overriding conclusion is that BMod is an eye-opener. It frequently gives us fascinating insights into why people behave as they do at work, and, in doing so, often suggests that we need radically to rethink some of our current man-management practices.

In particular, I have emphasized certain guidelines for the practising manager:
- The need to reward the right behaviours rather than to punish the wrong ones.
- Short-term pay-offs are more effective than long-term ones.
- Managers are responsible for performance, not for satisfying people's needs.
- Managers should manage individuals, not people *en masse*.
- BMod enhances coaching and appraising.

69

Now that we have seen how BMod can solve specific people-problems (Chapter 4), throw light on why they are so prevalent (Chapter 5), offer practical guidelines for the management of people (this chapter), it is time to look at some of BMod's theoretical underpinning.

7. *The new approach: some background, theory and basic principles*

So far I have introduced you to a version of BMod that I have developed over a five-year period. In this short chapter, I want to underpin the approach by showing you something of its lineage stretching back over a 120-year period of intense experimentation and controversy. So, in this chapter, I shall do some name-dropping and also permit myself to use the odd bit of behavioural-science jargon here and there.

Obviously, this is not the place for a detailed account of the theories and principles; if you want to explore the subject in more depth, then I will suggest some further reading at the end of this chapter. If you are inclined to take the theory on trust because you are interested solely in the *practice* of BMod, then by all means skip this chapter and go straight on to the next. However, if you read it, you will find that this chapter does give plenty of practical examples to illustrate both theory and basic principles.

So where does BMod come from? What are its basic principles? How many corners have been cut off to make it a palatable approach for the practising manager?

The version of BMod that I have described really emerged in two distinct phases. Initially, 120 years ago, attention was centred almost exclusively on what happened to elicit a response, or, in BMod parlance, how cues triggered behaviour. This work resulted in the cue → behaviour part of the BMod formula. Later, other people investigated the effect of reinforcement on behaviour and, eventually, this led to the second half of the BMod formula: behaviour → pay-off. So BMod, as we know it today, combines two areas of study and experimentation. Let us have a look at the background to see how BMod has emerged in its present form and then, in the second half of the chapter, examine basic principles.

The background of BMod

It all started in 1860 with a Russian called Ivan Sechenev (1829–1904). He was the first person to query the assumption that our behaviour originated in the mind. He distinguished between pure reflex actions, like eyes blinking and knees jerking, and 'complicated acts', but claimed that all man's achievements were 'associations between consecutive reflexes'.

Hard on Sechenev's heels came a host of people with all the paraphernalia of properly conducted experiments—controlled and uncontrolled variables, hypotheses and ingenious apparatuses of various kinds. Probably the best known of these was Pavlov (1849–1936), with his famous experiments on conditioning.

Actually, Pavlov was interested primarily in the study of digestion, and he received a Nobel Prize for his work in 1904. During the course of his experiments on digestion, he noticed that dogs secreted saliva *before* food was given to them. At the age of 50, and with some reluctance, he turned his attention to how this phenomenon came about.

Pavlov conducted hundreds of rigorous experiments. Broadly, they took the following lines. He paired a stimulus that did not naturally elicit the reaction of salivating, say a bell ringing, with one that did, such as the presentation of food.

After the bell and the food had been paired a number of times, Pavlov found that the dogs would salivate in response to the bell alone. The bell (or its equivalent, for Pavlov used a variety of stimuli in his experiments) was called the conditioned stimulus and the food the unconditioned stimulus. The sequence of events is represented in Figure 7.1.

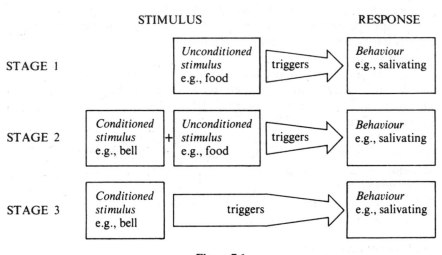

Figure 7.1

Pavlov repeated experiments like this, using different stimuli and responses, many hundreds of times. During the course of these experiments, he made other discoveries about the conditioning process. For example, he found that conditioning was temporary; if the dogs' response to the conditioned stimulus (the bell) was not occasionally reinforced with the presentation of food, it tended to disappear. He called this 'extinction'. Conversely, he noticed that, after a response had been extinguished, it would spontaneously occur again from time to time. This suggested that the response, once acquired, was intact just beneath the surface even after it had apparently disappeared. He also studied the extent to which a conditioned response would generalize to other similar stimuli. If a dog had learned to respond to a bell, for instance, would it respond to similar sounds or would it discriminate between them?

Pavlov's conditioning experiments were conducted with animals, mostly dogs. An American psychologist, Watson (1878–1958), conducted an 'infamous' conditioning experiment on a child called Albert. Baby Albert was successively confronted with a whole variety of potentially frightening objects—a white rat, a rabbit, a dog, a monkey, masks with and without hair, burning newspapers, and so on. Disappointingly (for Watson), Albert never showed any signs of being frightened by any of them. Eventually Watson got Albert to start and cry when frightened by the sound of a loud gong. Watson then paired the stimulus of the white rat with the gong and, after a number of repetitions, Albert would whimper and cry at the sight of the white rat! What's more, this response generalized to other objects such as a Santa Claus mask, a fur coat, a dog and a rabbit! Unfortunately (for Albert), Albert's mother protested at this point and stopped the experiment before Albert could be reconditioned. Watson wrote a famous report on the experiment, reaffirming his belief that all behaviour was learned by conditioning. He then quit and finished his working life as an advertising executive! (There must be a moral there somewhere!)

The theories of Sechenev, Pavlov and Watson all share one characteristic: they all emphasize the association between a stimulus and a response or, in BMod terminology, a cue and a behaviour. We now know that this is only half the story. So who was responsible for discovering the importance of the links between behaviour and reinforcement which led to the 'pay-off' idea being incorporated into BMod?

The first of the 'reinforcement theorists' was an American called Edward Thorndike (1874–1949). Like Pavlov, he worked with animals but his experiments followed a different design. A typical Thorndike experiment would follow these lines: a cat would be put in a cage, the door of the cage could be opened by pulling on a length of looped string. Immediately outside the door was a piece of fish. After wandering around the cage, doing typically cat-like things such as sniffing and scratching at the walls, it would eventually accidentally pull the string and the door would open. The cat was then free to eat the fish.

This sequence of events was repeated over and over again. As you would expect, the time between the cat being put in the box and opening the door got shorter and shorter. The cat had learned! But notice that this experiment, unlike Pavlov's, demonstrates the importance of reinforcement after the response rather than the stimulus before it. This led Thorndike to maintain that a response 'which is accompanied or closely followed by a reward will be strengthened and a response followed by "discomfort" weakened'.

Another American psychologist, Skinner (1904–), has extended the theories of Thorndike and others and is probably the most famous behaviourist to date. Skinner concentrates exclusively on observable events and does not theorize about the presence of any internal factors. Over the years he has conducted hundreds of detailed experiments to examine how reinforcers of various kinds sustain responses. For example, he has investigated the effects of different 'schedules' of reinforcement: if each response is followed by reinforcement, it is called a continuous schedule; if reinforcement only follows some responses, either at fixed time intervals or in ratio to the number of responses, it is called an intermittent schedule. Skinner has shown conclusively that intermittent reinforcement is more effective than continuous reinforcement. This, incidentally, is supposed to explain why gambling and games of chance are so gripping. In Skinner's terms, when we play with fruit machines, roulette wheels, bet on horses and play bingo, we are on an intermittent reinforcement schedule; in other words, we win intermittently rather than every time or never. Later in the chapter, when we look at basic principles, we will see how reinforcement schedules have been incorporated into modern BMod.

Skinner is also largely responsible for distinguishing between reinforcers in a way that has considerable significance for human behaviour. A reinforcer is anything that happens *after* the behaviour that encourages it, thus making it more likely to reoccur. Skinner, however, distinguishes between positive and negative reinforcement. Positive reinforcement occurs when, as you might expect, something rewarding follows the behavioural response; negative reinforcement, on the other hand, occurs when something unrewarding ceases following the behavioural response. Let me illustrate this by returning for a moment to the case of the husband with the nagging wife (see Chapter 1, page 2). Before a BMod strategy was applied to the problem, the wife was being positively reinforced because after she nagged, the husband knuckled down and fixed things. The husband, however, was being negatively reinforced because it was only after he had fixed things that the nagging (temporarily!) stopped. We shall return to the difference between positive and negative reinforcement later in the chapter when we look at basic principles.

Another important contribution to BMod by Skinner was his concept of shaping. In a series of fascinating experiments he has shown how it is possible to train animals (and people) by initially reinforcing rough approximations to the desired behaviour and then gradually tightening up until the required behaviour had been 'shaped'. It may sound flippant, but Skinner got pigeons to play ping-pong by successively shaping their behaviour from their first tentative 'accidental' pecks at a ping-pong ball. The shaping of behaviour has had important implications for contemporary BMod.

To illustrate this, let us take a simple case of bad timekeeping. You may find it difficult to see how to 'shape' more punctual behaviour; your first inclination is probably to stamp out bad timekeeping by punishing the offender, but later in the chapter we will see that this might not be advisable. If the latecomer is never punctual, how is it possible to use reinforcement? The answer is to settle initially for something short of perfect punctuality and use reinforcement to gradually shape the punctual behaviour. If the bad timekeeper is usually 30 minutes late, initially reinforce him when he is only 25 minutes late. Then successively tighten up to 20 minutes, 15 minutes, 10 minutes, and so on, until eventually he is reinforced intermittently for being punctual, or even 5 minutes early!

The major difference between Thorndike and Skinner and Pavlov and Watson is that the latter pair concentrated on searching for stimuli that evoked certain responses, whereas Thorndike and Skinner looked for re-inforcers that sustained the response. By combining the two, we have our BMod model, Figure 7.2.

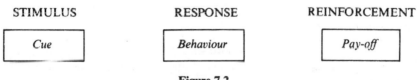

STIMULUS	RESPONSE	REINFORCEMENT
Cue	Behaviour	Pay-off

Figure 7.2

Stimuli, or cues, are important because they trigger the behaviour; re-inforcers, or pay-offs, are also important because they encourage the behaviour. In BMod we want to harness both.

Finally, to bring you right up to date, a word about developments during the last 20 years or so. There have been significant advances along two separate fronts. BMod has been increasingly applied to solving specific people-problems of the sort described in this book; in parallel with this, behaviour therapy, as it is usually called, has applied basic principles from conditioning and reinforcement to the treatment of behaviour disorders of various kinds. The behaviour therapists' list of abnormal behaviours that have been successfully treated is impressive and growing every day. Generally speaking they fall into four groups, as shown in Table 7.1.

Both behaviour therapy and BMod are based on the same fundamental assumption, namely, that behaviour, whether it be normal or abnormal, welcome or unwelcome, has been learned. The difference between behaviour therapy and BMod is not a difference of kind so much as of degree; whereas BMod concerns itself with relatively minor adjustments to 'everyday' people-problems, behaviour therapy is concerned with extreme cases of behaviour disorder. Behaviour therapy is for the highly trained specialist—BMod is for us all.

I hope that gives you enough background to understand how BMod has emerged from work on both the conditioning and reinforcement of behaviour. Now it is time to see how basic principles arising from this work have been integrated into the BMod approach.

Table 7.1

Behaviour	Examples
Fears and phobias	Fear of spiders, of flying, of the dark, of open spaces, of heights, etc.
'Neurotic' anxieties/ stress	Worry, migraines, impotence, high blood pressure, inability to relax, perfectionist obsessions, undue approval seeking, etc.
Destructive behaviour	Violence, vandalism, aggressiveness, etc.
Unwanted habits	Smoking, drinking, overeating, stuttering, etc.

The basic principles of BMod

The remainder of this chapter will pin-point four of the basic principles that have emerged from 120 years of painstaking research and been incorporated into BMod. You will see that some of the principles expand on points we have already discussed in earlier chapters, while others break new ground.

PRINCIPLE 1   THE CONTINGENCY CONCEPT

If you remember I discussed this in the last chapter (pages 60–62), so I will not dwell on it again now. Suffice to say that, if the gap in time between cue and behaviour, on the one hand, and behaviour and pay-off on the other is too long, then it is unlikely that associations between them will be made. In the last chapter I cited pay as a poor example of a contingent pay-off as well as giving other examples to illustrate the importance of this principle.

The other important strand in the contingency concept is the extent to which the pay-off is *conditional* upon performance. Skinner's work on schedules of reinforcement indicated that pay-offs need not happen *every* time the desired behaviour occurs; they should still be conditional, however, by never happening unless the desired behaviour has occurred. In the last two chapters I have suggested that, frequently, cues and pay-offs are unsystematically 'hit and miss' in many organizations. If pay-offs, in particular, are 'non-contingent', they cannot be expected to function as reinforcers of desirable behaviour. In other words, they will not work!

PRINCIPLE 2   BEHAVIOUR IS A FUNCTION OF ITS CONSEQUENCES

This principle arose directly from the work of Thorndike and Skinner, who concentrated, as we have seen, primarily on the links between behaviour and reinforcement.

This principle is perhaps the most important in the whole of BMod. But what exactly does 'behaviour is a function of its consequences' mean? Translated it means simply that behaviour is strongly *influenced by what comes after it*. This can happen in four different ways: two consequences increase behaviour, and another two decrease it. Let us look more carefully at how they function.

Positive and negative reinforcement

The two consequences that *increase* behaviour are called reinforcers and are split into positive and negative. We touched on this distinction a little earlier when discussing Skinner's work. You may find the idea of negative reinforcement difficult to comprehend; this is partly because it sounds paradoxical: how can reinforcement be negative? It is also because, in the same incident, one person can be positively reinforced while the other is simultaneously negatively reinforced. I will be giving an example of this complex 'dovetailing' of both sorts of reinforcement in a moment.

It is worth clarifying the difference between positive and negative reinforcement because they are both consequences that have a considerable influence on human behaviour. The difference between them is that positive reinforcement is 'nice' when it happens, while negative reinforcement is nice when it stops. Figure 7.3 may help to illustrate the essential differences between the two sorts of reinforcement.

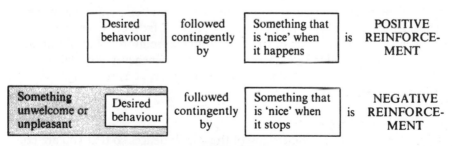

| Desired behaviour | followed contingently by | Something that is 'nice' when it happens | is | POSITIVE REINFORCE-MENT |

| Something unwelcome or unpleasant — Desired behaviour | followed contingently by | Something that is 'nice' when it stops | is | NEGATIVE REINFORCE-MENT |

Figure 7.3

So positive reinforcement is anything that happens (contingently) after the desired behaviour that is *welcomed* by the recipient, while negative reinforcement is something *unwelcome* that happens before or during the behaviour and only ceases when the desired behaviour has occurred. Both types of reinforcement *increase* the frequency of the desired behaviour.

To clarify further the difference between the two, let us look at an example. Suppose your boss asks you for suggestions about how a particular problem could be solved (the cue) and you immediately respond with some ideas (the *desired* behaviour). If your boss listens, agrees with your suggestions and even adds to them, providing *you* found this 'nice', your behaviour of putting forward ideas has been *positively reinforced*. In similar circumstances you are, therefore, more likely to come forward with ideas again.

On the other hand, if your boss kept chasing you for ideas and generally putting the pressure on you until he got ideas that he considered satisfactory, then, providing you found the pressure 'nasty' and its cessation 'nice', your behaviour of putting forward ideas has been *negatively reinforced*. Notice that your *boss*'s behaviour of chasing you and putting the pressure on is likely to have been positively reinforced, i.e., it was 'nice' *for him* when you finally came up with ideas that he found satisfactory. So, at the same time, your behaviour is being negatively reinforced and your boss's behaviour positively reinforced.

Punishment and extinction
The two consequences that decrease behaviour are called punishment and extinction. Punishment is the opposite of positive reinforcement in that it is 'nasty' when it happens. If, in the example we have just been discussing, your boss totally disagreed with your ideas and rejected them out of hand, then, assuming you found this unpleasant, your behaviour of putting forward ideas has been punished. This would make you *less* likely to behave like this in similar circumstances in the future.

Extinction, like punishment, also decreases behaviour, but does so less drastically. If, after you had put forward your ideas, your boss completely ignored them and moved on to consider other matters, your behaviour of putting forward ideas has been 'put on extinction'. Extinction is when *nothing* happens as a consequence of the behaviour, no reinforcement, no punishment—literally nothing. So, strictly speaking, whenever you deliberately choose to ignore an aspect of someone's behaviour, you are trying to reduce it by using extinction.

Combination strategies
It is often useful to combine some of the consequences so that you are contingently reinforcing the desired behaviour while punishing or extinguishing the undesirable behaviour. We have already seen lots of examples of this sort of combination strategy, and perhaps we can now recognize them as such. The husband with the nagging wife was using *positive reinforcement* when she asked him once, and *punishment* when she persisted in nagging. He positively reinforced her by committing himself, there and then, to undertake the maintenance task on a certain date noted in his diary; however, if she

nagged, he punished her by postponing the agreed date and making her wait longer for the maintenance task to be carried out.

Similarly, if you look back to pages 27–48, you will see that combination strategies were being used by the personnel manager with the 'stroppy' shop steward, by Ron with his 'circumventing' boss, by Rick with 'pouncing' Ian, and so on. Combination strategies are especially effective because they tend to contrast vividly the advantages of the desired behaviour over the disadvantages of the undesirable behaviour. The whole idea in applying BMod is to use a combination strategy to emphasize the positive pay-offs. The negative aspects need to be handled with kid gloves, since research shows that punishment, while often effective in influencing behaviour, has all sorts of unwanted side-effects. This brings us to the next BMod principle.

PRINCIPLE 3   REINFORCEMENT IS MORE EFFECTIVE THAN PUNISHMENT
Over the years psychologists have designed many experiments, some ingenious, some crude, to investigate how punishment influences behaviour. You have probably seen pictures on television from time to time showing animals cowering in corners, the unhappy victims of experiments into the effects of punishment. Distressing though these sights are, the experiments have at least given us useful data on the relative advantages of reinforcement over punishment. Punishment has at least two well-documented, thoroughly substantiated disadvantages. Let us briefly look at each in turn.

Punishment only temporarily suppresses behaviour
Evidence shows that punishment only temporarily suppresses behaviour rather than permanently changing it. As many exasperated parents and teachers have discovered, when the punishment, or the threat of it, ceases, the old behaviour tends to pop up again! The only way to ensure that the unwanted behaviour does not reappear is to keep it dampened down by a continuous programme of punishments. So punishment tends to lead to more punishment.

To illustrate the fact that punishment only temporarily suppresses behaviour, consider the following incident. Imagine you have an office with large windows looking out over an open-plan office; through these windows you can see what your subordinates are up to. You notice time and time again that one of them keeps reading a newspaper instead of working. Knowing that this particular subordinate is sensitive to criticism, you decide to reprimand him in the open-plan office where many of his colleagues at neighbouring desks will hear what is going on. After you have done this, you are pleased to notice that he does not read the newspaper again.

From your point of view, the punishment exactly fitted the crime and has been totally effective in stopping the unwanted behaviour. This successful experience makes it more likely that you will use public reprimands again in similar circumstances in the future. Your punishing behaviour has been positively reinforced and, naturally, you conclude that public reprimands work!

But do they? Certainly it appears so, since you did not see the subordinate reading his newspaper again. However, if it were possible to keep careful watch over a longer period, you would discover two interesting things. Firstly, whenever you were absent from your office, the subordinate would very probably read his newspaper—in effect, the subordinate has merely learned not to read his newspaper when you are around! This is obviously not the rip-roaring success you imagined it was. Secondly, in the absence of further punishments, the subordinate would gradually slip into reading his newspaper again, even when you were around. This is because the pay-offs he gets from reading the newspaper as opposed to doing his work remain unimpaired by your public rebuke. In these circumstances, you have two choices: either you must find some way to link working to pay-offs, or you must keep punishing the newspaper reading. The former is positive and likely to be more effective in getting him to work; the latter is negative and likely to be less effective.

Punishment leads to unwanted side-effects
The second disadvantage of punishment as opposed to reinforcement is that, rather like potent drugs, it leads to unwanted side-effects. It is very likely that the subordinate you publicly rebuked for reading his newspaper will:
– use every opportunity to tell everyone what a swine you are.
– waste time and energy plotting how to get his revenge.
– engage in minor, or even major, acts of sabotage that will inconvenience you.
Presumably, none of these reactions would be welcomed by you; the punishment that appeared so successful at first sight has back-fired.

Even though reinforcement through pay-offs is much more effective than suppression through punishments, this does not mean that punishment needs to be abandoned altogether; we have already seen how it can be built into a combination strategy as second fiddle to positive reinforcement. The over-riding conclusion about the use of punishment is that you should understand how it influences behaviour and use it as part of a *considered overall strategy* rather than on a haphazard, uncoordinated basis. Even then, you need to be alert for unwanted side-effects. The following quote from a newspaper report says it all: 'Managers of an American store chain who fell from grace had, it is reported, peanuts shoved up their noses and custard pies thrown in their faces and were obliged to run backwards through their own shops. The group went bust.'!

80

PRINCIPLE 4 INTERMITTENT REINFORCEMENT IS MORE EFFECTIVE
THAN CONTINUOUS REINFORCEMENT

Empirical research has shown conclusively that the timing of reinforcement
has more effect on behaviour than the size of the reinforcer. So a small pools
win could be just as effective in reinforcing your 'coupon-filling' behaviour
as a big one, providing you won frequently enough. Surprisingly, intermittent reinforcement, which does not reinforce every response, tends to
promote stronger, more lasting behaviour than continuous reinforcement,
which always follows the behaviour. This is extremely convenient to the
practising manager because it means that he does not need to ensure that all
desirable behaviours are reinforced *every* time they occur; he must, however,
ensure that the desired behaviour is reinforced contingently and frequently
enough to encourage its continuance. Suppose, for example, you have a
secretary who is prone to typing at great speed and does not bother to check
for errors. You painstakingly encourage her to correct typing errors before
the completed work reaches your desk. If you warmly thank her every time
she produces an error-free piece of typing, you are using continuous
reinforcement.

She now *expects* warm thanks each time, but imagine that you now fail for
some reason or another to thank her three or four times in succession. Despite
your good intentions, this could easily happen if, say, you were involved in
complex negotiations at the time the typing was delivered at your desk and
you did not check it until after your secretary had left for home. The chances
are that uncorrected errors would return because of the sudden contrast
between continuous pay-offs and no pay-offs or extinction. Continuous
reinforcement is effective at maintaining the desired behaviour so long as the
pay-off always follows the behaviour; intermittent reinforcement, where you
thank your secretary warmly after she has brought you her fourth or fifth
piece of error-free typing, is not only more convenient for you, it is also
more effective.

Continuous reinforcement is particularly useful in the early stages of
attempting to modify behaviour. We have already seen that combination
strategies make a strong initial impact on behaviour because they highlight
the contrast between reinforcing and punishing consequences so effectively.
Once the desired behaviour has been established with continuous reinforcement, you can safely move over gradually to an intermittent schedule of
reinforcement. So, in the case of your secretary, you might *start* by thanking
her warmly each time she brought error-free work (and punishing her each
time it contained errors); when error-free work had become the norm, you
could thank her warmly every other time, then every fourth time and, finally,
perhaps every sixth time.

Obviously, the intervals between reinforcement must not become too long
otherwise the old unwanted behaviour will reappear. Also, it is vital not to

become so complacent that you start to *expect* error-free typing ('that's what she's paid for') and neglect to reinforce her at all; intermittent reinforcement must never be allowed to fizzle out.

The precise reasons why intermittent reinforcement is more effective than continuous reinforcement are complex and beyond the scope of this book. Broadly, they dovetail with the points I made in the last chapter about motivation. As we saw then, the behaviourists' view is that people behave to acquire what they lack. It follows, therefore, that we will tend to work harder to acquire pay-offs that we have not already got. Most of the behaviour we have acquired through a long period of *ad hoc* experimentation has been intermittently reinforced; the occasional good, straight, long drive by a golfer will keep him playing the game despite the many balls he loses in the rough in between. The occasional influential report will keep the O and M specialist hard at it despite all the flack he gets at other times; 'We can't win them all', we say, and try even harder.

The vital thing to remember about intermittent reinforcement is that, even though it does not happen every time the behaviour occurs, when it does it must be contingent. Earlier, I illustrated the importance of contingency by citing the case of the monthly salary cheque; you can now see that all payment systems are intermittent since no one ever gets handed money each time they do a small unit of work. But few payment systems are contingent. It is the combination of intermittent *and* contingent reinforcement that is so effective.

Summary and suggestions for further reading

In this chapter we have looked, very briefly, at the way BMod has developed from the first experiments into conditioning and reinforcement. We have also examined four basic BMod principles; these should obviously be heeded when using BMod to solve people-problems. Here are some useful questions you can use to check that they have been.

When you have devised your modification strategy ask:
- Are the gaps between the new cues, desired behaviour and new pay-offs short enough for the connections between them to be obvious?
- Does your strategy emphasize reinforcement (preferably *positive* reinforcement) over and above negative controls such as extinction and punishment?
- Does your strategy allow for moving from a continuous schedule of reinforcement (where you reinforce the desired behaviour each time it occurs) to an intermittent schedule (where you reinforce the behaviour conditionally but less frequently)?

At the start of the chapter I promised to suggest some further reading. Since I always find long reading lists 'punishing', I will restrict myself to mentioning just two short books. For those of you who are interested in reading more about the history of BMod from Pavlov right up to modern behaviour therapy, I suggest:

A primer of behavioural psychology by Adelaide Bry. Published by Mentor in 1975 in paperback (123 pages including a glossary of terms and a bibliography).

If your interest is less general and primarily about the application of BMod in organizations, then I suggest:

Organisational Behaviour Modification by Fred Luthans and Robert Kreitner. Published by Scott, Foresman & Co. in 1975 in paperback (204 pages including references and suggestions for additional reading).

There are literally hundreds of other excellent books, but either or both of these will get you off to a good start.

8. The new approach: limitations and objections

In Chapter 4, pages 40–41, I listed seven advantages of the BMod approach and promised to redress the balance by examining its limitations in this chapter. Just to recap, the seven advantages are:
- BMod is optimistic about the possibility of solving people-problems.
- BMod avoids the problem-solving cul-de-sacs into which internal routes tend to take us.
- BMod whittles down large, seemingly impossible problems to a manageable size.
- BMod encourages us to manage the external environment.
- BMod works where other approaches have been tried and found wanting.
- BMod can be used by anyone, anywhere in a hierarchy.
- BMod modifies observable behaviour and this makes it easy to verify.

In this chapter I will start by discussing some limitations of the approach and then move on to look at a number of objections to it. The *limitations* need to be understood because they put constraints on the use of BMod and help us to understand when and when not to employ it. The *objections* need to be aired, and preferably overcome, otherwise they act as barriers, preventing us from giving BMod a fair trial.

The limitations and objections included in this chapter typify those raised by people when they first come across the BMod approach. Their doubts and concerns obviously diminish as they gain experience in using the approach successfully. With continued use, the whole thing tends to fall into perspective and many aspects that initially strike us as problems of application simply disappear with practice.

Questions that I will answer in this chapter include:
- How restricting is the fact that BMod can only cope with one behaviour at a time?
- What happens if you want to help someone modify their behaviour but do not see them very often?
- How can BMod help us solve pressing problems that need immediate solutions?
- Is not BMod too superficial in that it deals with symptoms and not causes?
- Is BMod manipulative and unethical?
- Is it not unrealistic to expect the practising manager to be a behaviour modifier?
- Could BMod back-fire on us and lead to a worse situation than we started with?

– Does not BMod merely formalize what we already do naturally?
The idea of this chapter, therefore, is to help you recognize the limitations of BMod so that you will not have unrealistic expectations of what it can do, and to help you overcome some of the barriers that might otherwise prevent you from trying it.

Limitations of BMod

HOW RESTRICTING IS THE FACT THAT BMOD CAN ONLY COPE WITH ONE BEHAVIOUR AT A TIME?

We have already seen that the approach is geared to processing a single unit of behaviour. Earlier, I likened BMod to a slot machine that will only accept one coin of a certain size at a time, and we have already seen this in operation. If we return to the people-problem cases in Chapter 4 (pages 33–48), Rick, for example, drew up a list of the problems he had with Ian's behaviour and selected just one for processing; Ted did the same when thinking about his sales director's behaviour. It was easier for Bert because he had only one behaviour he wanted to modify in the first place.

On the face of it, processing one behaviour at a time is very restricting, and many of the persistent problems we have with people are large and pressing. It seems unlikely, for example, that the managers reporting to Ian would have had the patience to isolate just one of Ian's behaviours for scrutiny. They were under pressure of all kinds from Ian and would no doubt greet the suggestion that his style be broken down into specific units of behaviour with derision. The more urgent the problem, the more likely that those involved will find this an irritating constraint. In practice, however, the one-behaviour-at-a-time rule is not the limitation it first appears to be; often, when selecting the priority behaviour, we discover that it is intertwined with other behaviours on the list. Earlier, for example, we found that Rick could have taken any one of six of Ian's behaviours because they were so closely linked. Frequently, having successfully modified the most urgent of the unwanted behaviours, the others fade in significance or are indirectly influenced as the impact of the new behaviour 'spreads out' or generalizes. Ted's strategy for preventing his boss overloading him is a good example of this—if he succeeds in stopping the overloading behaviour, his strategy also makes it likely that his boss will turn fewer questions back and take more initiative in throwing light on the meaning of the data Ted discusses with him.

So a 'domino' effect frequently means that, in practice, BMod extends beyond the one behaviour it started with. However, we should not necessarily *expect* this to happen; BMod is a problem-solving technique designed to converge single mindedly on a carefully selected problem behaviour. The objective is quite specific: to replace the troublesome behaviour with a more satisfactory one. If, in achieving this, other problem behaviours diminish, that is a welcome bonus.

There is another reason why the one-behaviour-at-a-time rule is not as limiting as it first appears. In practice, the fact that BMod forces us to focus on a single unit of behaviour is often a positive advantage rather than a disadvantage. People-problems, particularly those that have developed over a period of time, are often so overwhelming in nature that it is difficult to see where to begin; in such circumstances, it is to our advantage that BMod concentrates on one issue. The likelihood of getting effective action is higher than if we tried to tackle everything simultaneously.

WHAT HAPPENS IF YOU WANT TO HELP SOMEONE MODIFY THEIR
BEHAVIOUR BUT DO NOT SEE THEM VERY OFTEN?
There is no doubt that BMod works best when we have regular and frequent contact with the person whose behaviour we wish to modify. This is because BMod involves arranging an environment where the person unlearns an old, unsatisfactory way of behaviour and learns a new or modified behaviour instead. As with any sort of learning, this takes time and requires a number of repetitions if the learning is to stick. Furthermore, we have seen that the modifier's* behaviour is so often an integral part of the strategy. Rick, Ted and Bert were all involved in the new cues and pay-offs, so, unless they had frequent contact with Ian, the sales director and Maureen respectively, they would not be in a position to exercise sufficient influence through the cues and pay-offs.

What is *sufficient* contact? In practice I have found a minimum of once every three working weeks to be viable; preferably, the contact would be more frequent than this. Bert had no problem since he saw Maureen every day, whereas Rick and Ted would need to arrange meetings on at least a three-weekly basis. This was not difficult, however, since in both cases the strategy required them to take the initiative. Once Rick had tested out the strategy a few times and reached the stage where he was confident enough to encourage his fellow directors to adopt a similar approach, his contact with Ian could lessen so long as his colleagues were using the strategy. What matters is how often the cue–behaviour–pay-off pattern can be repeated while the problem behaviour is being modified. It would not be crucial that Rick himself was always the instigator.

---

* As we get more involved with in-depth exploration of the BMod approach and its principles, I will increasingly need a way of distinguishing between the person who wants to help someone modify their behaviour and the person whose behaviour is being modified. I do not like the formality of the labels, but in future I will use modifier and modifiee as my shorthand. The *modifier* is the person who becomes aware of a problem with someone else's behaviour and seeks to analyse the situation and find a solution to the problem by modifying the other person's behaviour. The *modifiee* is the person whose behaviour is causing problems.

HOW CAN BMOD HELP US SOLVE PRESSING PROBLEMS THAT NEED IMMEDIATE SOLUTIONS?

People often express disappointment over the length of elapsed time between implementing a modification strategy and getting the desired results. Sometimes, the first time the new cues and pay-offs are applied there is a dramatic shift in behaviour; more usually, however, it takes a number of repetitions before making noticeable headway.

This is, of course, disheartening but it is important to remember that the sort of behaviours we are grappling with have developed over a long period of time. As we have seen, a basic assumption in BMod is that, apart from some reflexes, people have learned to behave as they do over a long period. Ian did not suddenly become 'autocratic'; the chances are that these patterns of behaviour had developed long ago, even before he became a manager. In effect, he had 'discovered' after many *ad hoc*, trial-and-error experiments that, when he behaved in certain ways, he got what he wanted, and when he behaved in other ways he did not. These experiences will have gradually hardened into a definitive style.

So the chances are that the behaviours *we* want to modify have developed over a long period. It is also likely that the behaviours in question have persisted in their present form, or something much like it, for a good while. Remember that BMod is at its most useful with persistent, apparently entrenched behaviour, and this means that we should employ it to make an impression on behaviour patterns that are virtually habitual.

All this means that the sort of behaviours we are tackling are going to take some shifting. We must *expect* the process to take time. Depending on the frequency of contact with the modifiee, it might take days, weeks or even months. Despite this, it should not require any investment of time over and above the contact we normally have, or should have, with the modifiee. Rick, for example, *should* have been seeking Ian's help with substantial problems; it was a sensible way to tap Ian as an important resource. Ted *should* have been comparing notes with his sales director on a more frequent basis, and Bert should clearly have been supervising Maureen's work more closely. The BMod strategies we devised for Rick, Ted and Bert all involved them in more frequent contact with their respective modifiees. In each case, however, it was time they should have been investing in the normal course of events and not something 'extra' over and above their duties.

The short answer to the question, then, is that BMod cannot help us solve pressing problems that need immediate solutions. It can give a *potential* solution after a few minutes of analysis and thought, and even implementation can *start* pretty well immediately, but seeing it through to a satisfactory conclusion is likely to be anything but immediate.

87

CONCLUSION ON LIMITATIONS

We have now looked at three limitations of the BMod approach:
- The one-behaviour-at-a-time rule.
- The need for sufficient contact between modifier and modifiee.
- That modifying persistent, often habitual, behaviour takes time.

Sometimes we have seen that these limitations are apparent rather than real. At other times, they have emerged as a mixture of both limitation and advantage. Of overriding importance, however, is that recognition of its limitations helps us to see how to use BMod appropriately; to be successful users we need to deal with specific units of behaviour, have sufficient contact with the modifiee and have sufficient patience to 'stick with it' over a period of weeks or months. I will be returning to this last point about the need for patience later in this chapter.

Objections to BMod

For the remainder of this chapter let us turn our attention to some of the objections that are commonly levelled at BMod. As we shall see, many of these are emotional rather than rational, but then objections often are!

BMod, in its short history, has a notorious reputation for getting itself misunderstood and provoking emotional outbursts of hostility. I do not believe we need look far to see why this is so; as we saw earlier when contrasting internal and external explanations of behaviour, the internal argument has an appealing, familiar ring to it. In a sense, it is more complimentary to us all to suggest that our behaviour springs from deep-seated emotions; it makes us extra special, very complex and 'human'. The external argument, by contrast, seems degrading. We rush to our own defence: 'Surely my behaviour isn't triggered by external events? I *decide* whether to react or not. Surely my behaviour can't be explained by short-term pay-offs? For one thing, I'm more far sighted and purposeful than that; for another, I'm not that selfish. My behaviour is frequently altruistic and where are the pay-offs in that?'

Conscious that it will be an uphill struggle, I want to face the objections to BMod in this chapter squarely and, where possible, help you to see how to overcome them.

OBJECTION 1   IS NOT BMOD TOO SUPERFICIAL IN THAT IT DEALS WITH SYMPTOMS AND NOT CAUSES?

This argument usually runs along the following lines: behaviour is an outward manifestation caused by inner events such as thoughts, motives, attitudes, beliefs, feelings or any combination of these; if someone is uncharacteristically irritable (outward behaviour), we attribute it to some inner cause—'He got out of bed on the wrong side this morning' or 'He isn't feeling himself today.' So strong is the assumption that behaviour is caused by underlying factors that, as we saw in Chapter 2, traditional approaches to solving people-problems all tend to set to work directly on motives, attitudes, beliefs or feelings and expect the overt behaviour to modify in response. There are numerous examples of this: managers trying to make people 'safety conscious' or to nurture feelings of loyalty towards the organization, trying to instil favourable attitudes to management policies, or to motivate people by meeting inner needs such as the need for self-esteem. Diagrammatically, the internal argument looks like Figure 8.1.

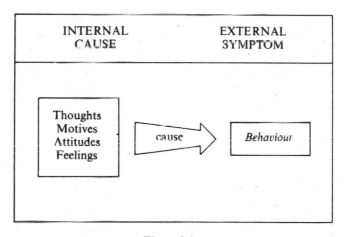

Figure 8.1

In contrast, the BMod approach focuses directly on overt behaviour itself and the external events which surround it. Just to recap, the BMod argument goes like this: apart from some reflexes, all our behaviour has been acquired through learning; this happens as we make 'connections' between external events in our environment and our behaviour. So, for example, a manager might learn to shout at subordinates when they argue with him because he has discovered a 'connection' between shouting and the cessation of arguments. He might agree with anything his boss suggests because he has learned to connect 'agreeing with bosses' with winning their approval. Alternatively, he might have learned to disagree with suggestions from his boss because he has discovered a connection between disagreeing and winning concessions. The crux of the BMod argument is that, if we have learned to behave by making connections like these, then learning will continue and modified behaviours emerge if the environment is rearranged so that new 'associations' are made. Figure 8.2 represents the external argument.

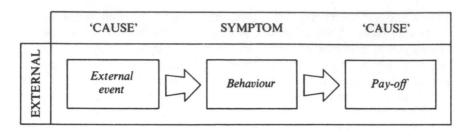

Figure 8.2

As we have seen, the approach virtually ignores internal events, and this gives rise to many concerns. It does not deny the existence of internal events so much as question their *relevance* to behaviour modification. No one doubts that thoughts and feelings exist; the difference between internal and external approaches centres on whether they play an important *causal* role in the occurrence of behaviour.

So *is* it superficial to concentrate on external rather than internal events? There are two possible answers.

The first is trite and dismisses the issue by arguing that, since BMod works, it does not much matter whether behaviour is caused by internal or external events. If you are a pragmatist, you will be content that BMod is successful in solving persistent people-problems and never mind how or why!

The second answer is that external events initiate both internal *and* external reactions. Cues trigger internal reactions such as thoughts, feelings, moods, attitudes and motives in just the same way that they trigger external behavioural reactions. No one just feels, say, irritable in a vacuum; something must happen to trigger the feelings of irritation. 'Getting out of bed on the wrong side' is a euphemistic way of acknowledging, not very precisely, that some event triggered both the irritable behaviour and its accompanying bad mood.

This means that we need to *start* by identifying external cues irrespective of whether it is behaviour or feelings we seek to modify. So, in effect, inner events as well as behaviour can be regarded as symptoms all 'caused' by external happenings in the person's environment. This helps us to see that inner events are often experienced in *association* with overt behaviour, but that it is a fallacy to maintain that they are necessarily causal. This wider picture is represented in Figure 8.3.

In Chapter 10 we shall look in more detail at the interplay between feelings and behaviour when we adapt the BMod approach in order to use it to modify our own behaviour and feelings. Suffice to say at this stage that there is plenty of evidence to suggest a two-way flow of traffic between feelings and behaviour. Take a simple example: suppose you are to give a talk to a large

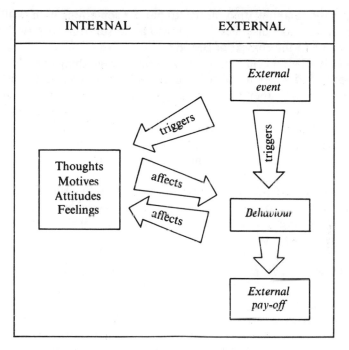

Figure 8.3

audience and you *feel* inadequate about doing it. Further, suppose you sub-sequently manage to behave in a competent, confident way, totally concealing the butterflies in your stomach. The chances are that your confident behaviour will have a knock-on effect to the underlying feelings and the butterflies will go away. This example shows that feelings of confidence are just as likely to come about as a *result of* behaving confidently as the other way round.

Far from being superficial, external events are the key to understanding both feelings and behaviour. As I have already promised, we shall return to this theme again. For now it is sufficient to understand that, irrespective of whether we wish to modify behaviour directly or indirectly, external events are an inevitable starting point. It is difficult to see how we can make a lasting impact on behaviour, attitudes, feelings or anything else without influencing the environment in which they occur.

OBJECTION 2 IS BMOD MANIPULATIVE AND UNETHICAL?
Manipulation is a strange, emotionally laden word; the context in which it is used makes a vast difference to its meaning. Thus it is good to manipulate the controls of a machine and bad to manipulate election results. Similarly, it is good to manipulate a strained back and bad to manipulate the market. On

the one hand, manipulation means 'to handle something with skill' and, on the other, 'to make dishonest changes so as to suit our purposes'. So what does it mean in the context of BMod?

Certainly, BMod is in business to help us change things but does it do so dishonestly and solely to suit our purposes? The answer is that BMod is a technique that is neither good nor bad; just like any other management technique, it is neutral. It is the *purpose* to which we put it as users that decides the issue. No doubt we could use BMod to make dishonest changes to suit our purpose but, for reasons I shall advance in a moment, it is much more likely to be successful in making honest changes in the interests of the modifiee.

There are really two issues here. One is: who benefits from the changes, the modifier, modifiee or both? The other is: are the changes brought about cunningly, without the modifiee's knowledge, or is it done openly with the modifiee's cooperation?

Let us take these in turn. First, who benefits? In all the examples I have given of BMod in action, I hope I have shown that both modifier and modifiee benefit. Considering the modifiee first, if BMod is done properly it virtually *guarantees* that the modifiee benefits, since pay-offs, in order to function properly, must be a satisfactory outcome for the *modifiee*. So Ian benefited by having problems fixed better and faster, Ted's director benefited by having more interesting sessions with Ted, and Maureen benefited by having longer lunch breaks and going home earlier. As we have already seen many times, pay-offs are a powerful ingredient in the BMod process and help to ensure that there are adequate advantages for the modifiee in altering behaviour. Satisfaction is guaranteed! If the pay-offs are not sufficiently beneficial, no change will take place.

The process is not one sided, of course—the modifier stands to gain as well. After all, the modifier is the person with the problem! He is using BMod to solve the problem and, if he is successful, that is clearly to his advantage. Rick got more helpful problem-solving responses from Ian, Ted got more mileage out of his director and was less overloaded, and Bert got the vouchers processed on time without drafting everyone in to lend a hand. But, as we have seen, these gains for the modifier are not at the expense of the modifiees. The overriding point about BMod is that both parties gain.

That brings us to the question of whether BMod is an essentially furtive process where the modifier schemes away in private and imposes a modification strategy on an unsuspecting modifiee. Certainly, it may initially strike you as an approach that is weakened if the modifiee knows what is going on. If, however, you see it as a way of solving problems with advantages to the modifiee as well as the modifier, it begins to look less like an exercise in one-upmanship. In Chapter 6 I showed how BMod could be used by both modifier and modifiee *together* as a useful way of structuring a counselling or appraising session. At this stage this may strike you as a little ambitious, and you may prefer to envisage going through the BMod steps on your own without conferring with the modifiee; although, at first, you may not be able to contemplate levelling with the modifiee, like anything else you will find it becomes easier as you become more confident in identifying cue–behaviour–pay-off links. Involving the modifiee brings all sorts of additional advantages—for one thing, they may be able to throw light on possible cues and pay-offs that are obscure to you. Also, their involvement is likely to enhance the process of change rather than inhibit it. If the new cues and pay-offs are well conceived, their potency will not be diminished because the modifiee is 'in the know!' The whole thing can be above board and the better for it.

What, then, about the ethics of BMod? Is it unethical to attempt to modify behaviour? If so, we are all guilty hundreds of times each day. Just think how often you try to exert influence over other people's actions, whenever you attempt to persuade, motivate or lead. Just about all your actions are aimed at influencing people in one way or another. Of course, it does not appear as blatant as it sounds in cold print but, like it or not, your behaviour has an impact on other people. Either we face up to this and accept some responsibility for the process or we can pretend that it is not happening.

Fascinatingly, I have noticed that the more people are encouraged to think about their behaviour, the more they care about ethics. Once the penny drops that your behaviour has an impact on other people, you are likely to become more conscientious in harnessing this process for their benefit as well as yours; it is no longer a question of letting rip just because you feel like it or blurting out whatever first comes to mind. And yet the tendency is to object that BMod, done thoughtfully, is unethical and done thoughtlessly is ethical! On balance, however, thoughtless behaviour causes more damage than thoughtful behaviour. So the question is whether the unwitting use of BMod is ethical while the deliberate, witting use of the same approach is unethical! The answer takes us back to earlier points about the neutrality of any tool or technique, including BMod. The ethics of BMod are less to do with whether the user employs the approach consciously or unconsciously and more to do with his purposes. If he seeks to gain an unfair advantage, he is using it unethically; if he seeks to gain mutual advantage, he is using it ethically. BMod is innocent. It is we, its users, who determine its reputation.

OBJECTION 3 IS IT NOT UNREALISTIC TO EXPECT THE PRACTISING MANAGER TO BE A BEHAVIOUR MODIFIER?

This question usually stems from a number of different but interrelated objections. Often there is a strong feeling that BMod is best left to the experts—whoever they are! Another strand is that BMod takes up time that busy managers do not have. Yet another is that BMod demands too much in the way of self-discipline and patience for many managers to contemplate. We shall examine these points one by one.

Firstly, should busy managers include the modification of people's behaviour among their duties? My answer to this is an unequivocal yes.

Managing is all about modifying. Managers are in business to modify, and maintain for the better, all aspects of their operating environment: money, materials and men. BMod fits into this perfectly since it focuses the manager's attention on the links between the working environment and the way people are behaving. I have tried to show that BMod is an entirely feasible way of tackling people-problems of various kinds. Even though they may be loath to admit it, most managers have their fair share of people-problems; BMod is a practical way of solving those problems. BMod is what the practising manager should be doing, deliberately and unashamedly.

The question remains, though, as to whether the actual activities involved in BMod are legitimate tasks for managers to be undertaking? Again, my answer is yes, they are. Fundamentally, BMod requires the manager to diagnose and prescribe; as the man on the spot, he is in a unique position to do both. He can diagnose unsatisfactory behaviour and the factors in the working environment that are affecting it. He can prescribe by working out what changes to make in the working environment to bring about behaviour modification in the required direction.

The only aspect that might strike the manager as novel and unusual is the accent on specificity and thoroughness rather than generalities and vagueness. As we have seen, BMod involves specifying a precise behaviour for modification and pin-pointing the links between it and cues and pay-offs in the environment. I am aware that these sorts of activities sound unattractive to a 'seat of the pants', impulsive manager. He would prefer to cut corners and deal in generalities, to think in terms of overall performance with words like 'loyalty', 'reliability' and 'flexibility'.

However, working at the level of precision required by BMod only requires the basic analytical skills many managers already employ when tackling other aspects of their work. BMod does not require an expert, merely a manager who is prepared to face up to his people-problems and solve them by using a disciplined BMod approach.

Does BMod demand extra time that busy managers do not have? I hope I showed earlier in this chapter that BMod does not require managers to do anything over and above the things they should be doing in any case when managing people. The actual business of analysing a people-problem the BMod way takes minutes, not hours, and often takes a shorter time than wrestling with the imponderables in other (internal) approaches. I know it often sounds like a feeble argument—especially if you are trapped in the vicious circle of reacting to immediate events—but using BMod to solve people-problems actually saves time in the long run. Significant problems eat up time both because they cause time to be used inefficiently and because people spend time complaining to each other about the problem; imagine the amount of unproductive time Ian's direct reports must have spent grumbling about their existence under Ian's regime!

It is true that the *elapsed time* between implementing a strategy and establishing a modified behaviour can be considerable, but this does not necessarily mean that, on a day-in, day-out basis, the modifier has to invest extra time.

Finally, is BMod unrealistic in the demands for self-discipline and control it places on managers? We have seen that BMod involves a methodical analysis of the problem and the application of a modification strategy, perhaps for a period of weeks or months. In all the examples we have considered, we have seen that the modifier is heavily involved in the strategy; if he forgets to implement a changed cue or forgets to use the planned pay-off, it can set back the whole process. This is clearly bad news for the rash and impulsive!

I shall return to the business of self-control in the final chapter and show how we can adapt the BMod approach to influence our own behaviour and feelings. Suffice at this stage to say that, in BMod terms, the self-control problem is a very real one; if the behaviours involved in self-control are not 'rewarded' with pay-offs, the model will predict that self-control will diminish. If our modifiee shows no perceptible change in the early stages of implementing the strategy, we are not getting our pay-offs and the temptation to give up will be very strong. In this case—recognizing the influence of pay-offs in shaping our own behaviour—we must be careful to arrange pay-offs to sustain us especially during the bleak period of no apparent change. This will be discussed further in the last chapter.

OBJECTION 4   COULD BMOD BACK-FIRE ON US AND LEAD TO A WORSE SITUATION THAN WE STARTED WITH?
There are usually two dangers envisaged by people when they first meet the BMod approach. One is that the wrong behaviour might be modified; the other is that, even if the right behaviour were modified, there might be unexpected and unwanted side-effects: 'You could finish up with a worse situation than you started with.' Let us take these in turn.

First, how likely is it that the wrong behaviour would be selected for modification? I think this is a remote danger. We would not even think of employing BMod until we had a persistent behavioural problem that had not responded to other forms of treatment; BMod is not concerned with one-off or infrequent problems. The persistence of the problem makes it unlikely that we will get it completely wrong. Furthermore, the technique itself encourages us to take great care when selecting the behaviour for modification. We have seen how all the disappointments with the modifiee's behaviour are listed and systematically filtered down so that we are left with the ones

95

most detrimental to the modifiee's performance. Admittedly, there is a judgement to be made here, but the specificity of the BMod approach helps us to make a sound decision rather than a rough-and-ready one.

Secondly, what are the dangers of BMod back-firing on us with unexpected side-effects resulting from the modified behaviour? We saw earlier that modified behaviours *can* generalize and have knock-on effects to other behaviours, but the knock-on effects are restricted to *associated* behaviours and, to this extent, they are unlikely to take us by surprise. Ian was a good case in point. If Rick could succeed in modifying his tendency to pounce and sort out problems himself, we saw that it might well knock-on to other associated behaviours on Rick's list, such as:
- Being a stickler for detail.
- Adopting an aggressive questioning style.
- Bawling people out in public.
- Interfering a great deal.

It is most unlikely, however, that curing Ian's tendency to pounce would result in surfacing other, more terrible tendencies in Ian. The BMod solution was not going to frustrate him because it was careful to ensure that he still enjoyed his pay-offs—but not by pouncing.

If, by any chance, we observed an undesirable side-effect following a successfully modified behaviour, all is not lost—it simply means we go back to the drawing board and do a fresh cue–behaviour–pay-off analysis on the side-effect behaviour. In practice, however, it is much more likely that we would be delighted with the knock-on effects of a modified behaviour rather than struggling to contain them.

OBJECTION 5 DOES NOT BMOD MERELY FORMALIZE WHAT WE ALREADY DO NATURALLY?

This is the 'it's just common sense' argument. It is certainly tempting to discount other people's solutions to their problems as obvious. It is easy to claim that we would never have got into that mess ourselves and, furthermore, that the solution was staring them in the face without the need for a problem-solving technique like BMod. However, a double standard frequently operates whereby other people's problems seem inconsequential while our own seem complex, even unique.

The whole point about BMod solutions to people-problems is that they must be feasible to the people who have to implement them—BMod is not in business to produce elegant, novel or exciting solutions, merely solutions that work. This means that a solution arrived at using BMod will often appear quite unremarkable to everyone but the problem owner. In real life, Rick, Ted and Bert were genuinely bowled over by the BMod solutions to their problems; the process and the answers it rendered certainly did not seem like common sense to them.

96

In my experience, BMod rarely produces a solution to a problem that the people involved were contemplating, far from it. The most widespread 'natural' reaction to the sort of entrenched people-problems we are concerned with seems to be to apportion blame and do nothing; it is always 'their fault' or 'the system's fault'. There are always numerous excuses for procrastination: 'It would create a precedent', or 'Personnel regulations don't allow it.' The BMod approach forces us to do at least two 'unnatural' things: the first is to examine the situation and see whether we, unwittingly, are instrumental in triggering the problem behaviour; the second is to put ourselves in the modifiee's position and search for pay-offs from their point of view. Both these activities are 'unnatural' in the sense that, without BMod as a guide, people simply do not do them.

CONCLUSION ON OBJECTIONS

We have aired five objections commonly levelled at BMod:

- The worry that BMod is superficial and deals with symptoms and not causes.
- The concern that BMod is manipulative and unethical.
- The objection that BMod makes unrealistic demands on busy managers.
- The worry that BMod could go wrong and make matters worse rather than better.
- The suspicion that BMod merely formalizes something we already do naturally.

No doubt there are more objections and I shall try to cope with these in the remaining chapters of the book. My aim at this stage is to have put each objection into perspective in such a way that you feel keen enough to give BMod a whirl! The next chapter gives you a chance to do just that; it contains six people-problems for you to solve using the BMod approach.

9. *Exercises for solving people-problems*

This chapter contains six people-problems that were solved using BMod. As before, the problems are all real; none of them has been invented. The idea is to give you the opportunity to test out your BMod 'prowess' before you 'go live' and apply the approach to some of your own people-problems. The chapter is in three sections:

1. A step-by-step routine you can use as a foolproof guide to analysing and solving a problem using BMod.
2. Descriptions of the six people-problems, each fairly brief but containing sufficient information to make it possible for you to solve them using BMod. The problems are in order of difficulty starting with the simplest.
3. The solutions that were implemented successfully in real life. There is no suggestion that the real-life solutions are the only, or even the best, solutions to the problems; they are offered merely to give you an interesting basis of comparison with your own solutions.

A step-by-step BMod routine

The routine that follows has been tested by hundreds of managers who, during the last few years, have used it to arrive at solutions to their people-problems. During that time the routine has evolved and, very gradually, been perfected. If you feel impatient with the rigidity of routines and procedures, then I recommend you to stick to it slavishly a couple of times and then decide what corners you can safely cut. If having cut corners things go wrong, you can always return to the routine for a while before launching out on your own again.

The routine comes in the two versions shown in Table 9.1. There is a full version that spells out what to do in considerable detail, and an abbreviated version that gives one-sentence instructions. If the abbreviated version is clear enough, do not bother with the full one; if you feel uncertain at any stage, read the longer version.

Table 9.1

Abbreviated version	Full version
1. List *all* disappointing behaviours.	Centre your attention on the person whose behaviour is to be modified and list the ways in which he behaves that you consider disappointing.

Table 9.1 *continued*

Abbreviated version	Full version
2. Cross out items that are not strictly behavioural.	Check that each behaviour you have listed is specific enough and actually describes something the person does overtly. Cross out the things you have listed that are not behavioural.
3. Cross out items that are not obviously related to job performance.	Check that each remaining listed behaviour actually impairs the person's current job performance. Cross out things you have listed that are not obviously related to job performance.
4. Select the single, most important disappointing behaviour.	If you still have a number of behaviours on your list to choose between, select one of them for processing through the remaining steps of this routine. Try to select the one which is most obviously detrimental to the person's job performance.
5. Write down the behaviour selected for modification.	Write down the selected behaviour on a sheet of paper; this is the behaviour you wish to modify. (Note: now that you have pin-pointed a behaviour you want to modify, in most cases this is as far as you should go on your own. Unless there are exceptional circumstances, arrange to go through the remaining steps jointly with the modifiee.)
6. Identify cues that trigger the disappointing behaviour.	Identify when the behaviour occurs by answering the question: 'What are the cues that appear to trigger the behaviour?' Write down the cues on the sheet of paper immediately above the behaviour.
7. Identify pay-offs that encourage the disappointing behaviour.	Identify what happens immediately *after* the occurrence of the behaviour that is currently a satisfactory outcome for the person. Do this by answering the question: 'What is it in the current situation that makes the behaviour so satisfying to the person?' These are the existing pay-offs. Write them down immediately under the behaviour.
8. Decide what behaviour you want.	Having identified the links between the behaviour you wish to modify, its existing cues and its existing pay-offs for the person, you are now ready to write down the behaviour that you wish to see in the person. This will usually be a reversal of the behaviour selected for modification at Step 5.
9. Check that the wanted behaviour is sufficiently beneficial.	Having described the desirable behaviour, check that it is likely to result in sufficient improvements in performance. Do this by listing the performance-related benefits that you anticipate the desired behaviour will lead to. If you are clear that the modified behaviour will result in a satisfactory number of performance improvements, work out a modification strategy by proceeding with the subsequent steps. If, however, you are uncertain that the desired behaviour defined in Step 8 will result in sufficient improvements in

99

Table 9.1 *continued*

Abbreviated version	*Full version*
	performance, abandon it and select a new required behaviour that meets more of the anticipated benefits/needs.
10. Work out how to alter the cues to: – encourage the wanted behaviour, and/or – discourage the disappointing behaviour.	Decide whether it is feasible to change the cues by looking back at the cues you identified in Step 6 and answering the question: 'Is there anything I/we can do to alter the existing cues so that the likelihood of the existing behaviour is decreased and the likelihood of triggering the desired behaviour is increased?' List any actions you can think of.
11. Work out how to alter the pay-offs to: – encourage the wanted behaviour, and/or – discourage the disappointing behaviour.	In addition, look at the existing pay-offs identified in Step 7 and answer the question: 'Is there anything I/we can do to reinforce the desired behaviour immediately after its occurrence, and/or to discourage the existing behaviour immediately after its occurrence?' List any actions you can think of.
12. Select a feasible modification strategy.	Finalize your modification strategy by selecting the actions from Step 10 and/or Step 11 that you feel you are able to commit yourself to. When making your selection, continually check whether it is feasible for you to implement the strategy. (It will not work unless you can 'stay with it' perhaps over a long period.)
13. Work out how to implement the strategy.	Consider how to launch your modification strategy. For example, if you have not already done so, would it help to be open with the person about your strategy? If not, it may mean that, regrettably, it is more appropriate to implement the strategy quietly, without prior discussion.

Six people-problems

This section contains six descriptions of people-problems. Use the BMod routine, either the abbreviated or full version or a combination of both, to solve them. Remember that the problems are in order of difficulty. If you feel confident, you might like to start with Problem 4 and then tackle 5 and 6; if you feel more hesitant, tackle Problem 1 first and then decide which, if any, to skip. The real-life solutions are given in the last section of the chapter on pages 107–112.

PROBLEM 1   ROBERT—YOUNG SCIENTIST
Robert is a young scientist working on a research problem in a large Research and Development organization. He has a degree in mathematics and is in his first job, so he is a 'green' graduate. Generally speaking, he is much happier

with 'things' than with people, but some of the problems he is encountering are beginning to get him 'hooked' on the 'human element'—an aspect he has always ignored before.

As a graduate scientist he does not have any *direct* subordinates, but his work does mean he has to share some centralized services with other colleagues. In particular, he is dependent upon a couple of programmers since an important part of his work involves computer analysis of the results of experiments using a very complicated new code. The code was 'invented' by someone else and does the job excellently, the only snag being that it is difficult to learn. There are two girls who prepare input data to the computer for Robert's part of the organization; both girls have the reputation of being willing programmers and they have the necessary qualifications and experience.

When Robert first started to put experimental data in that required the use of the new code, the girls naturally found it difficult. They had a bit of a moan about the complexities of the code and Robert sympathized and suggested that they try to learn the code during slack periods. This was not an unreasonable suggestion since there are fairly frequent intervals, in a typical week's work flow, when things are quiet on the data preparation front. Furthermore, Robert tried to impress on them the need to conquer the code at this early stage, and explained that the frequency of jobs requiring the new code would increase rapidly in the near future.

Robert was disappointed to notice that his suggestion was not taken up, however, since the girls seemed to prefer to knit in slack periods rather than take any initiative in learning the new code. Accordingly, Robert had a word with his boss with the aim of getting him to impress the need to learn the new code on the girls in readiness for the increasing number of jobs that will require the new code. After a week or so, the boss told Robert that he *had* mentioned it to the girls and was confident that, in future, they would busy themselves learning the code during slack periods.

During the next few weeks Robert was again disappointed. So far as he could see, the girls continued to knit and chat during slack periods rather than master the new code.

Robert is now extremely puzzled about what to do next. He wonders whether he should have another go at the girls. Alternatively, should he try to enlist his boss's help again?

Using the BMod approach, what would you advise Robert to do to modify the girls' behaviour during slack periods? (The solution Robert successfully implemented, Figure 9.2, is given on page 107, see how your solution compares with his.)

PROBLEM 2   SALLY AND HER DISAPPEARING BOSS
A secretary named Sally worked in a large office block in a room adjoining

101

her boss's office. Her boss was a senior manager and a conscientious man who had the maddening habit of disappearing, sometimes for long periods, without telling Sally where he was going. He seemed to do this 'at the drop of a hat', usually after receiving a telephone call or piece of correspondence that had posed a problem that he could sort out at once by having a word with those involved.

His disappearances caused Sally considerable embarrassment. When people telephoned or dropped in during one of his absences, she had to confess that she did not know where he was or when he would be back. If something urgent cropped up, she rang around trying to locate him and, besides taking time, this earned her the reputation of being an inefficient secretary. She listed less urgent messages and had them ready on his desk waiting for attention when he returned.

She greatly resented the embarrassments and the snide remarks people made, such as: 'What, lost him again then?' and 'I'm surprised you don't handcuff him to his desk!' Sally was a meticulous, orderly person who hated uncertainty and untidiness. Time and time again she had remonstrated with her boss, begging him to tell her where he was going *before* he went there! He always agreed that this was desirable and apologized for causing her problems, but soon relapsed and carried on in exactly the same fashion.

Sally decided to work out a way of solving the problem. Clearly, asking him to tell her merely where he was going was inadequate. Short of locking the door from her boss's office into the corridor, thus forcing him to come through Sally's office on his way out, what can Sally do to modify her boss's behaviour? (Sally's solution to this problem, Figure 9.3, is given on page 108.)

PROBLEM 3   ROY AND HIS OVERDEPENDENT SUBORDINATE
A personnel officer called Roy heads a personnel department in a manufacturing company. The department is quite small: there are three personnel assistants, two record keeping clerks and two typists. One of the personnel assistants, a man called Harold, is in charge of the general office. This is a place where all the personnel records are kept (of which there are many), where all the personnel documentation is processed (of which there is much), and where anyone in the company can drop in with personnel-type queries. There is an enquiry counter in the office which even has a bell on it to ring for attention.

As you can imagine, people troop in with all sorts of queries, some substantial and some trivial, all day long. One of Harold's jobs is to give on-the-spot interpretations of such things as conditions of service, personnel regulations, employment legislation and the like. Over the years, he has become something of a walking encyclopedia about such things. He is fond of rattling off obscure 'small print' just to impress people with his grasp of it all.

So far, so good. Unfortunately, Harold has a serious shortcoming; whenever a query comes from management that requires Harold to make a decision about the precise interpretation of a procedure or regulation, he always balks, avoids making a decision and refers it to Roy. Harold is fine at dealing with the more cut-and-dried queries that do not require interpolation, interpretation or judgements, but he is not at all keen on coping with 'shades of grey'.

Roy is concerned about the credibility and reputation of the personnel department and, when Harold refers one of these decisions to him, Roy goes ahead and makes it as the most expedient thing to do in the circumstances. Whenever he does this, however, he is vaguely aware that, in doing so, he is actually encouraging Harold to continue being overdependent.

At a recent appraisal discussion, Roy talked through the problem with Harold, but Harold explained that he needed to have Roy's support in this way because so many dire consequences can result from an unfortunate misinterpretation. Precedents can so easily be created which have a knock-on effect over a long period; the company could lose large amounts of money. In the discussion, Harold admitted that in the past he had had his knuckles rapped for making precedent-creating interpretations off his own bat without getting them 'signed off' by higher management.

Roy is left wondering what he can do to get Harold to take more decisions without referring. (Roy's solution, Figure 9.4, is given on page 109.)

PROBLEM 4   DOROTHY AND HER RETICENT GROUP

Dorothy is manager of a division and has nine managers reporting to her. The nature of the work means that these managers are spread geographically. For example, the four senior line managers are based in quite different places: one in Northern Ireland, one in Glasgow, one in Manchester and one in London. The remaining managers reporting to Dorothy provide the usual services to the line (Personnel, Marketing Services, Comptroller, etc.) and they are split between London and Manchester.

Once a month the whole group meet in London. They refer to themselves as the executive group and typically start their monthly meetings at 11.00 hours, have a working lunch, and usually finish by 17.00 hours. These hours of work allow far-flung managers to fly to and return from the meetings within the same day.

Habitually the executive group start with a briefing session where Dorothy passes down information she has gleaned from a monthly staff meeting she attends, convened by her boss, and then moves on to a working session where they tackle an assortment of agenda items. Sometimes these require someone to give a mini-report on a designated subject area; other agenda items are more 'open ended' and require on-the-spot reactions from everyone. One of the declared objectives of the executive group is 'to cause ideas to develop more creatively than would come from individuals alone'.

When Dorothy first took over as manager some two years ago, she tried to adopt a participative style; she found this difficult because she tends to be a woman who does not suffer fools gladly and has high standards about the competence of those about her. She particularly prides herself on being a logical, analytical thinker. She has developed this over many years and this largely explains why she has been so successful in a 'man's world'. Her analytical skills are so entrenched that she is intolerant of anything based on 'gut feel' or intuition.

Unfortunately, her tendency to favour analytical thinking above all else interferes with the generation of more creative off-the-top-of-the-head ideas in herself and others. This means that she tends to analyse most ideas to death, particularly if they are wild or creative, by pointing out faulty logic and/or why the idea is not practical. Gradually, this has had the effect of reducing the number of suggestions from members of the executive group.

Things have now got to the stage where suggestions from the group are hardly forthcoming; try as she might to solicit them, the group tends to hang back waiting for Dorothy to produce a suggestion herself. Dorothy privately complains that the group is overdependent on her and resents their reticence. The group members reckon that Dorothy is too autocratic and is not genuine in inviting their contributions; they are suspicious of her, feeling that, even though she asks for their suggestions, she has already made up her mind. As one of the group said, 'If she has already made up her mind, why pretend she hasn't? In my view, she doesn't change her mind often enough for me to believe that she is prepared to.'

What can Dorothy do to rejuvenate her executive group and encourage them to join in problem-solving agenda items? (Dorothy's solution, Figure 9.5, is given on page 110.)

PROBLEM 5   DICK, THE DP MANAGER

Dick is a data processing manager in a manufacturing company. He manages a DP department some 25 strong with three direct reports, as shown in Figure 9.1.

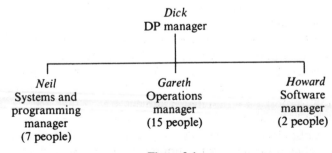

Dick
DP manager

Neil
Systems and
programming
manager
(7 people)

Gareth
Operations
manager
(15 people)

Howard
Software
manager
(2 people)

Figure 9.1

Dick has been DP manager for four years; his three direct reports were all appointed from within by him and have been in post for about two years. Dick is not happy with the quality of interaction between his three managers. The sort of thing that disappoints him is that they argue between one another in front of third-party managers, they express divided opinions in meetings with users, they do not exchange information and tend to keep secrets from one another, and they pass the buck and blame each other for failures to meet deadlines, etc.

The buck-passing has been on the increase just lately because the DP department has been under pressure to introduce some new systems. Dick has noticed how, as deadlines come and go at different stages of the project, Neil in particular keeps blaming Gareth or Howard, and even Dick himself, for not doing their part. The sniping has resulted in verbal punch-ups at their weekly review meetings with, on some occasions, the meeting being abandoned in disarray.

Dick has had independent sessions with Neil where he tried to get him to commit himself to firmer target dates (he prefers to leave things 'open' if possible), but Neil always becomes very resistant, objecting that he cannot commit himself to a specific target because Gareth and/or Howard and/or Dick and/or someone else are bound to let him down on the parts of the job that involve them. If necessary, he will even hark back to poor decisions of the past saying, 'I told you they shouldn't have put that machine in back in '73.' Reactions like this are even more violent whenever Neil has actually failed to meet a target date, he lashes out at everyone and everything and never ever concedes any blame or failure on his part.

Dick decides that he must get a grip on the situation. Ironically, he can see that Neil's behaviour has meant that he tends to lay off Neil and put more pressure on Gareth and Howard; Gareth and Howard are resentful of this and accuse Dick of pussy-footing with Neil. Dick starts by listing all the things Neil does that he considers disappointing. When he has finished, his list looks like this:
- He fails to cooperate with Gareth and Howard.
- He blocks innovatory suggestions made by others.
- He is difficult to handle in meetings.
- He 'sulks' if he does not get his own way.
- He does not work well under stress—particularly to tight deadlines.
- He avoids blame by accusing others.
- He will not commit himself to target dates, preferring to leave things vague and open.
- He never admits to a mistake or failure.
- He withholds information that ought to be shared.

With such a daunting list, Dick wonders how to go about improving Neil's behaviour. Not surprisingly, he is tempted to get rid of him, but rejects this

105

option because Neil is an excellent systems man from a technical standpoint, and there is no one in the department competent to replace him yet.

Using the BMod approach, what strategy would you advise Dick to adopt? (Dick's solution, Figure 9.6, is given on page 111.)

PROBLEM 6   DAVID AND ALEX

David is manager of a warehouse. It has a total head count of 300 people, a management team of 9, including David, a gross stock-holding of £18 000 000 and approximately 60 000 part numbers. David reports to Alex, who works at headquarters some 100 miles distant and has a number of warehouse managers, such as David, reporting to him.

David had been drafted in as manager 18 months ago specifically to sort out a number of complex problems that are bugging the warehouse's performance. The warehouse had a shocking record of avoidable human errors. Sending the wrong parts to the wrong places at the wrong time were virtually daily occurrences, as was not having required parts in stock even though the demand patterns were predictable. However, David soon starts to realize that his biggest problem is not managing the warehouse so much as managing Alex: 'My biggest problem is a total lack of support from Alex. I am constantly subjected to overt and covert criticism for things I haven't even done. He is much too dependent on glib tales from his lieutenants at HQ. I act more confidently and successfully when I'm encouraged by, not congratulations, but by an attitude that indicates that I'm doing a pretty sound job. Under these conditions I take better risks and chances and have more successes. I'm far more hesitant when I feel I'm failing. I'm more careful and stop arguing. I tend not to fight back when people criticize.'

David feels that Alex is hypercritical and never supportive, often plain rude, unreasonable and does not understand David's problems. He complains that Alex often contacts David's subordinates direct without David knowing and intermittently descends on the warehouse, taking over David's office for the duration of his stay. David is at his wit's end knowing how to cope with the considerable task of sorting out the warehouse problems with no help from what amounts to a 'hostile' boss. He wishes that Alex would consult him more and give him more encouragement and support.

Alex is an ex-army Ordnance Corps Brigadier. He was recruited by the organization a year ago to sort out considerable problems in the network of warehouses; the biggest warehouse is managed by David. Alex is under increasing pressure from his bosses to get the warehouses performing more efficiently. Alex is a meticulous man and is becoming impatient for discernible improvements. After six months or so, it starts to dawn on him that David is his biggest problem; he complains: 'David is too secretive and doesn't consult me enough. He keeps problems to himself until it is too late and, when they are 'discovered', he always has excuses. I don't like doing it, but in-

106

creasingly I find the only way to find out what is happening is to circumvent David and go straight to his subordinates. Either that, or get my HQ chaps to poke around and winkle the information out for me.'

What can David do to improve relationships with Alex? (David's solution, Figure 9.7, is given on page 112.)

Solutions

This section gives the real-life solutions to the six problems just described. They are a useful basis of comparison with your solutions. If your solutions differ, they are not necessarily wrong; there are no right or wrong solutions. It is worth noting, however, that the real-life solutions were all implemented successfully and so they were found to be adequate in practice.

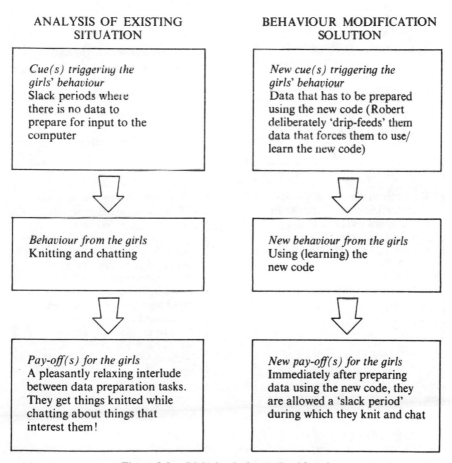

Figure 9.2. BMod solution to Problem 1

ANALYSIS OF EXISTING
SITUATION

BEHAVIOUR MODIFICATION
SOLUTION

*Cue(s) triggering the boss's
behaviour*
Telephone calls or items of
correspondence that pose
problems he can sort out at
once by having a word with
those involved

*New cue(s) triggering the boss's
behaviour*
None. Sally could not think of a
feasible way of altering the
existing cues.

Behaviour from the boss
Leaves his office without telling
Sally where he is going or how
long he is likely to be

New behaviour from the boss
Tells Sally where he is going
and gives an estimate of how
long he is likely to be

Pay-off(s) for the boss
He solves the problems quickly.
He is tracked down if something
urgent crops up. Less urgent
problems are listed for him in his
absence and are on his desk when
he returns

New pay-off(s) for the boss
None, but now the existing pay-
offs are contingent upon the
new behaviour. When he
'disappears', Sally reverses the
pay-offs by tracking him down
with trivia and saving urgent
problems. (In real life, Sally
only applied these sanctions
twice before bringing about a
permanent change in his
behaviour; it simply was not
worth his while to 'disappear'
without telling her where he
was going)

Figure 9.3. BMod solution to Problem 2

ANALYSIS OF EXISTING
SITUATION

BEHAVIOUR MODIFICATION
SOLUTION

*Cue(s) triggering Harold's
behaviour*
Queries from management that
require him to make a decision
about the precise interpretation
of a procedure or regulation

*New cue(s) triggering Harold's
behaviour*
Whenever Harold refers a decision
to Roy, Roy involves Harold in the
interpretation of the procedure and
the correct decision

Behaviour from Harold
He balks, avoids making a
decision and refers it to Roy

New behaviour from Harold
He does the interpreting and
makes the decision

Pay-off(s) for Harold
Roy obliges and makes the
decision. Harold avoids any
unpleasant repercussions

New pay-off(s) for Harold
Roy gives his interpretation and
decision unreserved support. Roy
says he will back him up if there
are any unpleasant repercussions.
Harold finds that, more often than
not, managers are grateful for his
'wise' advice

Figure 9.4. BMod solution to Problem 3

109

ANALYSIS OF EXISTING
SITUATION

BEHAVIOUR MODIFICATION
SOLUTION

*Cue(s) triggering the group's
behaviour*
Open-ended agenda items where
Dorothy solicits on-the-spot
reactions from everyone

*New cue(s) triggering the
group's behaviour*
Dorothy categorizes agenda items:
1. Items where she has already got
   a preferred solution which is
   only open to slight modification.
2. Items where she has some ideas
   but wants the group to help her
   select the best one.
3. Items where she has no ideas at
   all and wants the group to join
   her as equal partners starting
   from scratch.
For items in Category 3, Dorothy
imposes brainstorming rules: 'think
wild, cross-fertilize, suspend
judgment, go for quantity, not
quality'

Behaviour from the group
No suggestions/reactions —
they hang back waiting for
Dorothy to produce a suggestion
herself

New behaviour from the group
They pitch in with lots of
off-the-top-of-the-head ideas

Pay-off(s) for the group
They avoid having their ideas
'analysed to death' by Dorothy.
They 'force' Dorothy to come
forward with her own ideas, which
they can then react to (less
'risky')

New pay-off(s) for the group
Their ideas are actively
considered/listened to. They 'enjoy'
being free to cross-fertilize/think
wild, etc.

Figure 9.5. BMod solution to Problem 4

ANALYSIS OF EXISTING SITUATION	BEHAVIOUR MODIFICATION SOLUTION
Cue(s) triggering Neil's behaviour When Neil has failed to meet a target date and/or when Dick tries to get Neil to commit to a target date	*New cue(s) triggering Neil's behaviour* When a target date has slipped, Dick goes to Neil, and, in effect, takes the blame for setting an unrealistic target date and suggests they review the situation together

Behaviour from Neil Accuses others/never admits to a mistake or failure	*New behaviour from Neil* He talks over the situation constructively, without accusations and without going defensive

Pay-off(s) for Neil Avoids blame. Dick lays off Neil and puts more pressure on Gareth and Howard	*New pay-off(s) for Neil* He continues to avoid blame. Dick puts less pressure on him when he is constructive (*but*, if the old behaviour occurs, Dick deliberately steps up both blame and pressure)

Figure 9.6.   BMod solution to Problem 5

ANALYSIS OF EXISTING SITUATION	BEHAVIOUR MODIFICATION SOLUTION

Cue(s) triggering Alex's behaviour
A shortage of information from David about problems/progress at the warehouse

New cue(s) triggering Alex's behaviour
David telephones Alex at least once each day to consult him about a problem and/or to update him on a problem that might escalate and/or to report successes

Behaviour from Alex
Contacting David's subordinates direct and/or sending his 'lieutenants' in to winkle out the information

New behaviour from Alex
He gives David more advice/help as well as giving him more encouragement and support

Pay-off(s) for Alex
He gets the information he craves. He can use it to stave off the pressure from his boss to get the warehouse performing efficiently

New pay-off(s) for Alex
He more easily gets the information he craves, straight from the 'horse's mouth', and has earlier warning of potential problems. He is better able to stave off pressure from his boss

Figure 9.7. BMod solution to Problem 6

Conclusion

If you have used the BMod routine on at least three of the problems in this chapter, then you should be ready to use it on some of your real-life people-problems. I hope you have discovered that it is worth while disciplining yourself through the steps of the routine and that, with practice, it is becoming more 'automatic'. Try not to take too many liberties with the routine, however; remember that it encapsulates the accumulated experience of literally hundreds of managers. They found it *worked*!

Now that we have seen how to use the BMod routine for the solution of the problems caused by other people's behaviour, in the last chapter we will look at how to use the approach for the modification of our own behaviour.

10. *How to modify your own unwanted behaviours and feelings*

So far, this book has been about how to solve the problems caused by *other people's* behaviour. In this chapter I shall show you how you can use the same basic approach to modify *your own* behaviour, and even to modify your own *feelings*. The essential feature, therefore, is that this chapter is all about *you* and how you can use BMod on yourself. The advantage of being able to do this is that you are better equipped to take full responsibility for your own actions and development; ultimately you, and you alone, are accountable for your own behaviour and BMod is a considerable help in facing up to this fact and doing something constructive about it.

The chapter starts by examining the major differences between applying the BMod approach to yourself as opposed to other people, and then goes on to show how you can extend the basic approach to modify those feelings that adversely affect your behaviour.

How to use BMod on yourself

As you have seen in earlier chapters, a basic tenet throughout BMod is that we have all acquired our various behaviour patterns over a long period of *ad hoc* experimentation. In a rough-and-ready way, behaviours that stood us in good stead we have retained; behaviours that got us into trouble we have dropped. All this has happened in a fairly unsystematic way and it is unlikely that you have given the process much conscious thought.

If we are to control our own behaviour, we need to do it more consciously and systematically than we are accustomed to, and this is where the BMod approach offers a helpful framework. Modifying our own behaviour requires us to go through similar steps to those required when modifying someone else's. All the ground rules we have explored in earlier chapters apply: the importance of selecting one specific problem behaviour, the careful search for cues triggering it and pay-offs encouraging it, and, finally, thinking out feasible ways of changing the cues and/or pay-offs so that the problem behaviour decreases and is replaced by a new, more satisfactory behaviour.

Despite the fact that cues, behaviours and pay-offs remain the basic ingredients there are four significant differences in applying BMod to yourself. We will examine each in turn.

DIFFERENCE 1   IDENTIFYING WHAT BEHAVIOURS TO MODIFY

You are much more likely to be aware of the problems caused by other people's behaviour than the problems caused by your own. Even when in everybody else's opinion you have made a mistake with your behaviour, you may have a different view and/or rationalize the mistake away. This makes it much more difficult to identify what behaviours to modify. As we have seen, the first five steps of the BMod routine are all concerned with the identification of a specific behaviour that is sufficiently detrimental to job performance to warrant BMod attention (see Chapter 9, page 99). The first step of the routine starts with the listing of all your disappointments with the modifiee's behaviour. But what if you are simultaneously both the modifier and the modifiee? How can you identify disappointments with your own behaviour?

Here are four suggestions to help you recognize which of your behaviours would benefit from modification:

1. Whenever you fail to produce desired results, *assume* that the failure resulted from mistakes you made rather than being caused by other factors that were 'beyond your control'. Conduct a careful post-mortem of your own actions and compile a list of all the things you could have done differently. The list provides a starting point for BModing yourself.

2. Even when you succeed in producing desired results, periodically review your own actions and list what you could have done even better. Often you know in your heart of hearts that you are capable of performing better, and your own disappointments with yourself are an important information source and an excellent starting point for BMod.

3. When you are disappointed with the way other people react to you, assume (even though it may not be true) that it is your fault. So when people do not listen to you, do not adopt your suggestion, do not consult you, etc., assume that your behaviour was at fault, not theirs. This forces you to scrutinize your own behaviour rather than blame other people.

4. On the rare occasions when people criticize you and offer you explicit feedback about your behaviour, accept it gratefully rather than springing to your own defence. Feedback is easier to accept if you can do something constructive once you have got it; if you know how to apply BMod to yourself, you are more likely to welcome feedback when it is offered and also more likely to solicit it actively. Other people's perceptions of us are there to be collected if only we can pluck up the courage to ask for them.

Sometimes, of course, you are already only too clear about aspects of your behaviour that you would rather do without. Many 'bad habits' fall into this category: many people would rather not smoke, bite their nails, talk too much, be so reticent, be compulsive eaters and drinkers, and so on. In these cases, the difficulty is not with identifying the problem behaviour so much as in knowing what to do to change it.

115

DIFFERENCE 2 IDENTIFYING CUES AND PAY-OFFS FOR YOUR OWN BEHAVIOUR

The second difference when applying BMod to yourself rather than other people is the business of identifying cues and pay-offs. You might find it difficult to step outside yourself with sufficient objectivity to search for the external events surrounding your behaviour; knowledge of your internal experiences will tend to confuse the issue and give you additional problems in seeing the wood for the trees. I will return to the linkages between your internal feelings and your external behaviour as the basis for the fourth difference. The fact that you have access to your inner feelings is such a crucial difference between you and other people that the bulk of this chapter will be devoted to examining how to modify feelings that tend to hinder your behaviour.

Meanwhile, here are two 'tips' to assist you in identifying the external cues and pay-offs that sandwich your behaviour. Firstly, keep notes for a period to help in pin-pointing when the behaviour occurs; it is simply a question of noting down what happened immediately before you used the behaviour in question. Eventually, a pattern should emerge and you then have identified the cue. This note-keeping technique has been used very successfully in behaviour therapy to identify cues triggering 'bad' habits such as compulsive smoking or eating, and it works equally well for any type of problem behaviour.

Secondly, you might like to consider enlisting the aid of a friend or colleague to help you search for the cues and pay-offs surrounding your problem behaviour. The other person does not need to be involved in any way—in fact, it is probably best that they are *not* and have no 'axe to grind'—but they should be prepared to act as a sounding board. It is obviously extremely helpful if they are familiar with the BMod routine and, in particular, able to distinguish between external and internal events.

DIFFERENCE 3 IMPLEMENTING YOUR OWN BMOD STRATEGY

Another difference when using BMod on your own behaviour is disciplining yourself to stick to the modification strategy once it has been worked out. This can be an uphill struggle, as you may already have found when trying to break bad habits single-handed. The key to success is to have a *feasible* modification strategy rather than something that looks good on paper but is unrealistic in practice. In other words, your strategy must be a plan that you can adhere to doggedly, perhaps over a few weeks or months.

The most onerous part of the plan to manage by yourself is undoubtedly at the pay-off end of the formula. You should be clear how you are going to reward yourself *after* you have behaved as you wished. In a sense this is easier to do for yourself than for other people since you already know from experience what activities you find rewarding. A useful idea when it comes

116

to identifying rewards for yourself is to draw up your own personal list of pay-offs. Then, when you are devising a modification strategy, you can look down the list and select a pay-off that you will be able to reward yourself with.

The pay-off list must obviously be your own personal list, since it is vital that you find the items on it genuinely rewarding. However, just to give you an idea of what a pay-off list looks like, here is one of mine. This is my 'at work' list; I have a separate 'at home' version, since the sort of pay-offs that are feasible at home may not be at work, and vice versa!

- Reading the newspaper
- Reading an article in a journal
- Meeting up with X for lunch
- Putting the finishing touches to a report I have written
- Having a brain-storming session with X
- Bouncing original ideas off colleagues
- Preparing a presentation
- Drafting visual aids for a presentation
- Writing articles for publication
- Working out how to communicate something complex
- Looking at a John Piper painting/lithograph
- Gossiping about X with Y
- Speculating about developments with X
- Doing figure work with my calculator
- Doing a piece of technical/professional work

The items on your pay-off list must obviously be things that you can indulge in on your own initiative at work because you must be able to reward yourself *contingently*; the whole idea is to use your pay-offs on an 'If—then' basis. For example, '*If* I get these 'phone calls made, *then* I'll put the finishing touches to my report', '*If* I clear my in-tray, *then* I'll spend five minutes looking at a John Piper lithograph', or '*If* I proofread the progress report, *then* I'll bounce my ideas about so-and-so off X.'

I have found this simple system an excellent antidote to procrastination— we understandably tend to postpone tasks that we find tedious in some way. The 'If—then' routine ensures that the tedious but important tasks get done *first*, before we tackle things that we find more satisfying.

DIFFERENCE 4   MODIFYING INNER FEELINGS AS WELL AS OUTWARD
BEHAVIOUR

The final difference between using BMod on yourself as opposed to using it on other people arises from the fact that you have access to your underlying feelings. This means that you are able to take the feelings that accompany your behaviour into account, and this opens up the exciting possibility of tackling both problem behaviours and problem feelings in parallel.

The inclusion of feelings at this late stage may surprise you since, in earlier

117

chapters, I encouraged you to concentrate on overt behaviour and steer well clear of deeper-seated aspects, which included feelings. However, this sudden attention to feelings is not in any way inconsistent with that earlier advice. The reason why feelings are included here hinges on the fact that this chapter is all about *you*, whereas earlier chapters have been primarily about other people. A major difference between you and anyone else is that you, and you alone, experience your inner feelings; you cannot experience anyone else's, nor can anyone else experience yours. So if this chapter is concentrating on *you*, then it is perfectly sensible to show you how to modify your own unwanted feelings as well as your unwanted behaviour. This is only possible because you have access to your feelings; you cannot modify other people's feelings because you do not have direct access to them, which is why this book, until now, has concentrated first and foremost on behaviour.

Since the basic BMod approach concentrates exclusively on external events, we are going to have to extend the model if it is to encompass internal feelings as well as behaviour. The remainder of this chapter will, therefore, be devoted to showing you how the BMod approach can be extended so that you can use it to modify your unwanted or unproductive feelings.

How to modify feelings that hinder your behaviour

Feelings such as anger, boredom, happiness, worry, jealousy, excitement, guilt, fear, and so on can roughly be divided into three categories: those that help you to function effectively, those that hinder you and those that do not affect you either way. In this chapter I am going to concentrate on unwanted feelings that hinder you. *You are hindered whenever you are in a state in which you are not functioning at the level you would like to.* Feelings of anger, worry, guilt, and so on are only useful if they provoke you into doing something effective; unfortunately, such feelings often tend both to be unpleasant to experience and to hinder behaviour. You are hindered, for example, when:

- You cannot talk candidly with someone, even though you want to, because you feel too vulnerable or embarrassed.
- You cannot settle down to work on a project, even though it interests you, because you feel inadequate.
- You do not join in some enjoyable activity because of a gnawing feeling that you ought to be working.
- You cannot introduce yourself to someone who appeals to you because you are afraid of a rebuttal.
- You cannot think clearly because you are so irritated or angry.
- You cannot sleep because something is bothering you.
- You cannot say what you want to say because you are so nervous.

At first, the idea of modifying feelings that hinder behaviour strikes most people as extraordinarily novel. If you are finding it difficult to accept either the possibility or desirability of modifying your unproductive feelings, you are probably making some assumptions about them that need double checking.

Here are four assumptions that may be preventing you from tackling your unwanted feelings.

ASSUMPTION 1   ALL FEELINGS ARE INSTINCTIVE RATHER THAN LEARNED

Some internal experiences *are* instinctive in the sense that they were there from the word go—the sensation of the heart pounding and the adrenalin flowing when we are afraid, for example. Instinctive sensations are built into the system and are triggered automatically in certain situations.

The majority of the feelings we experience, however, are not instinctive at all. Just like behaviour, they have been acquired over a long period of *ad hoc* learning. You were not born worrying or feeling guilty or bored, nor were you born feeling inadequate or nervous. These are feelings which develop as you are exposed to different experiences; things happen and gradually we learn to associate external happenings with internal feelings. Eventually the learning is so thorough that it seems as though external events automatically trigger inner feelings. This, as we shall see, is not inevitable; we can consciously intervene in the process.

ASSUMPTION 2   FEELINGS CANNOT BE CONTROLLED, THEY JUST HAPPEN TO YOU

If you believe this, it would mean you were a zombie with no responsibility for how you felt. You would be completely at the mercy of other people and events, and believe they were entirely to blame for your feelings. In this chapter I hope to challenge this depressing view by suggesting that, if so many of our feelings have been acquired through learning, then we can continue to learn, unlearn, adapt, modify, update, replace and do anything we like with them. Feelings are just as amenable to modification and change as behaviour is.

ASSUMPTION 3   YOU SHOULD SUPPRESS YOUR FEELINGS

This suggests that inner feelings should be contained and not allowed to be reflected in outward actions. In our society this is a strongly held belief, since many feelings (of hostility and aggression, for example) are not considered desirable or 'civilized', so we are taught to suppress them. Sometimes this is helpful, of course, but the snag with suppression is that it only affects outward behaviour and does nothing to remove the inner feelings. Experiencing the feeling without expressing it puts stresses on you that can eventually result in unwanted side-effects; nervous breakdowns, ulcers, coronaries, headaches and backaches often result from intolerable stresses trapped between inner feelings and outward behaviour.

119

ASSUMPTION 4   YOU SHOULD OPENLY EXPRESS YOUR FEELINGS AND
TO HELL WITH THE CONSEQUENCES

Applied indiscriminately, this could get you into a lot of unnecessary trouble! This assumes that we have feelings that *must* be released through outward expression. It is obviously not socially acceptable or expedient to let behaviour be entirely dictated by feelings, which is why the suppression strategy above is so widely adopted. Expressing feelings may well avoid the penalties of suppressing them, but is likely to trigger adverse reactions in other people. You could even finish up in jail!

I am going to challenge these assumptions about the nature of feelings and show that they are inaccurate. They are also unhelpful because they encourage us to shift the responsibility for our feelings onto other people; while this is a convenient rationalization ('it's not *my* fault'), it blinds us to the possibility of managing our own feelings.

So let us replace these erroneous assumptions, or myths, with some *facts* about the nature of feelings—facts that open up the exciting possibility that you can modify feelings that hinder your behaviour.

FACT 1   MOST FEELINGS ARE NOT INSTINCTIVE, THEY ARE ACQUIRED

There are different schools of thought on the precise balance between instinctive and acquired feelings, but all agree that most of our major inner experiences have been acquired as a result of a lengthy learning process. Take the feeling of jealousy, for example. Studies show that people describe quite different emotional experiences under the general heading of jealousy; this suggests it comes in many different brands and sizes rather than being built into our innate system of reflexes, body chemistry, gene structure and the like. Furthermore, anthropological studies in cultures quite different from our own reveal that some cultures produce people who are entirely free of jealous feelings.

So there is evidence to suggest that many of our feelings are learned. This opens up the whole possibility of 'unlearning' the feelings that hinder our behaviour.

FACT 2   FEELINGS ARE INTERNAL REACTIONS TO EXTERNAL EVENTS
THAT YOU CHOOSE TO HAVE

So many of our feelings are ingrained and habitual that you may not be aware that you can exercise choice. But, if you think about it, you will realize:
– that none of your feelings happens in a vacuum—they are *always* preceded by an external event and by a conscious thought.
– that you can choose what feelings to have in relation to an external event. No one can *make* you feel anything emotionally—no one, nor any event, can *make* you feel angry, for example. You can choose whether to *feel*

120

angry in just the same way that you can choose whether to react angrily. It takes practice to get the choice mechanisms working again. In most people, they have lain idle for so long that it takes deliberate, conscious thought processes to stir them into action. More about how to do this later.

FACT 3   THE REASON WHY YOU CHOOSE TO HAVE UNPRODUCTIVE
FEELINGS IS BECAUSE YOU HAVE LEARNED THAT THEY HAVE 'PAY-OFFS'
FOR YOU

Sometimes the pay-offs are rather obscure and often self-destructive, but the fact remains that we learn to experience a feeling not merely in reaction to some outside event, but also because in the past it has resulted in a satisfactory pay-off for us. We shall see that people often retain feelings that hinder them because they are comfortingly familiar (you can enjoy being miserable), and often provide a convenient excuse for not taking action.

It will not have escaped your notice that these facts about feelings echo all we have previously said about behaviour: both external behaviour and internal feelings have been learned, both occur in response to external events or cues, and both anticipate satisfactory outcomes or pay-offs. This means that, if we extend our basic external model of cues → behaviour → pay-offs, we should be clearer about the linkages between external and internal events. In the case of feelings that hinder behaviour, the extended model can be represented by Figure 10.1.

Here is an example to illustrate the sequence through these six boxes.

1. External cue. Imagine I am attending a meeting where I am expected to

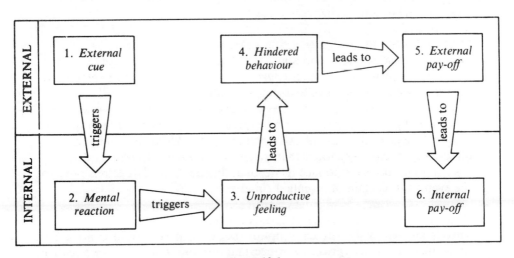

Figure 10.1

121

    contribute as some sort of specialist or expert. All the other attendees are more senior than I. I have sat through a couple of agenda items that have not concerned me; it is now my turn. I have got a novel idea to put to the meeting.

2. Mental reaction. My thoughts are something like this: 'They all look as if they know what they are talking about. They are more senior, more experienced, more capable than I. I wonder if my idea is good enough? They will probably tear it to shreds. They are bound to make mincemeat of me. . . .'

3. Unproductive feeling. Anxiety, i.e., butterflies in my tummy, heart pounding, breaking out in a sweat, etc.

4. Hindered behaviour. I put forward my idea in a hesitant way, hedging it with lots of ifs and buts. I start by saying: 'I may have got it all wrong but . . .' and finish with: 'I don't expect it will work but I throw it in for what it's worth. . . .'

5. External pay-off. While I put my idea they listened politely; now I have finished, I am relieved to find that they do not pick my idea to pieces so much as ignore it altogether. There are one or two half references to it, but soon their discussion regains momentum and they seem to have forgotten me and my idea altogether.

6. Internal pay-off. Great relief! 'They didn't criticize me. My anxiety has gone. I put my idea and they chose to ignore it. What else can I be expected to do? If they can't spot a good idea when it's laid before them, that's their funeral.' Pearls before swine, etc.

I will return to this example and show you how the unproductive feeling of anxiety could have been modified so that it did not hinder the behaviour. But, first, let us look at the options open to us.

OPTION 1   AVOID OR CHANGE THE EXTERNAL CUES

This is identical to the BMod approach. The argument goes like this: since the whole sequence of events is triggered by an external cue of some kind, identify the cue and arrange to avoid or change it.

    This is attractively simple and, as we have seen in BMod, it works. If we could avoid going to meetings in an expert capacity where we fear that our ideas will be given a rough ride, so much the better. Unfortunately, it is often impossible to avoid situations that trigger unproductive feelings and, in any case, it might be better to face them squarely and control your reactions to the events rather than the events themselves.

OPTION 2   REPLACE THE MENTAL REACTION

This is an extremely attractive option because, if we could control the thoughts that occur between the cue and the onset of the unproductive feeling, the feeling need never happen at all. This is a truly preventive option.

Besides being attractive, replacing the thoughts that trigger our unproductive feelings is also a very practical option. It may not appear so at
first because the passage of time has fused together cues, thoughts and feelings so that they seem quite indistinguishable. However, all our feelings are
heralded by thoughts, however fleeting, and we can learn consciously to
replace the thoughts that trigger unwanted feelings with other thoughts that
do not.

The snag with this option is that it requires you to be rational and let your
'head rule your heart'; paradoxically, this goes against the grain with the
people who need to do it most! The more you tend to be an emotional person,
the more you are likely to reject this option as unhealthy, unnatural, unethical, impossible or all four!

OPTION 3   SUPPRESS FEELINGS THAT HINDER BEHAVIOUR

Suppression is not so much a way of modifying the unproductive feeling as
of modifying its outward expression. The idea is to suppress the feeling so
that it remains an internal experience and does not manifest itself in behaviour. To some extent we all do this already since, as we were saying
earlier, the socialization process trains us to have 'a stiff upper lip' and not
express our feelings in an open, straightforward way. As a result, some people
are already skilled at hiding their feelings behind a behavioural façade.

The snag with this option is that the suppressed feelings are still experienced internally rather than avoided or prevented. A further difficulty is that
repeated mismatching between feelings and behaviour can build up stresses
in the system to the extent that something has to 'blow'. Bottling up feelings
is generally condemned as an unhealthy practice; the resultant stress can be
released either by learning to express our feelings more frequently and more
candidly or by using the next option.

OPTION 4   RELEASE THE UNPRODUCTIVE FEELING HARMLESSLY

As we have just seen, the problem with suppressing unproductive feelings is
that psychological and physiological stresses build up. When we feel angry,
for example, involuntary responses increase our blood pressure, heart rate,
rate of breathing, blood flow to the muscles and metabolism, preparing us for
conflict or escape—all systems are 'go' to react angrily. Our natural physiological mechanisms have put us in a state of alert and prepared us for what is
called the 'fight-or-flight' response. The problem is that fight-or-flight behaviours are less and less appropriate in today's civilized society and, if we
repeatedly suppress these feelings, they contribute to furred-up arteries, high
blood pressure, coronaries and strokes. Clearly, we need some harmless way
of releasing these pent-up feelings—relaxation techniques.

Experiments have shown that many of these techniques result in a state of
consciousness quite unlike being awake or asleep. The state has been des-

cribed as one of 'restful alertness' and it has shown that the heart rate decreases, metabolism is lowered, breathing rate decreases, blood pressure is lowered and brain waves change pattern.

So relaxation techniques are an important way to release unproductive feelings and, if you use the techniques regularly, to help put you in a better frame of mind so that you are not so vulnerable to unproductive feelings in the first place.

OPTION 5   CHANGE THE PAY-OFFS

Feelings, the argument goes, have been acquired (learned) over a long period of time. Roughly what happens is that we retain and repeat feelings that lead to satisfactory pay-offs for us and drop feelings which do not. At first sight, it may be difficult to square this explanation with the existence of unproductive feelings—surely, if they hinder behaviour, the feelings would not have been acquired in the first place? Unfortunately, unproductive feelings are frequently linked to satisfactory pay-offs that sustain and encourage them. For example, feeling put down and ignored could lead to the behavioural reaction of sulking, which frequently succeeds in getting people to pay attention to you. This external pay-off could make you *feel* better. People have frequently acquired feeling/behaviour patterns of this kind and use them to blackmail people into compliance. Also, many people wallow in unproductive feelings as a sort of kinky way of enjoying themselves—some people get kicks out of feeling small, rejected, lonely, clumsy, and so on. So we see how internal pay-offs do much to sustain even unproductive feelings. Furthermore, in the absence of more obvious external pay-offs, the sheer *familiarity* of unproductive feelings may be enough to guarantee their repetition after a while.

So this option involves discovering what pay-offs the unproductive feeling is linked to and arranging to break the link by replacing the existing pay-offs with new pay-offs. In effect, you are unlearning one linkage and re-learning another one in exactly the same way that you do when applying BMod to yourself.

As we shall see, this is quite the most difficult of the options to put into practice. Identifying external pay-offs involves a significant chunk of the BMod approach. Identifying *internal* pay-offs is even more difficult to do on your own; you may need someone to act as a sounding board if your internal pay-offs are to be pin-pointed with sufficient clarity.

These, then, are the options available to us. They are not mutually exclusive, of course; you can choose to use them all if you wish and, if you combine them with BMod, that gives you a grand total of six. Figure 10.2 shows them mapped onto the extended model.

124

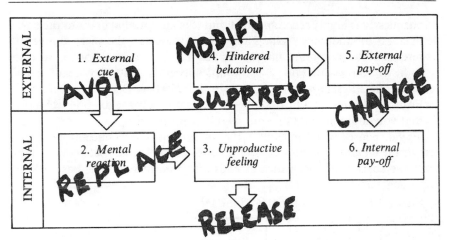

Figure 10.2

For the remainder of this chapter I am going to concentrate on three out of the six:
- Avoiding external cues.
- Replacing mental reactions.
- Changing external/internal pay-offs.

These three, as we shall see, are the mainstays of an approach to modifying unproductive feelings that is called Feeling Modification, or FMod.

I am not going to give as much attention to the other three options for the following reasons:

1. The option of directly modifying the hindered behaviour has already been dealt with extensively in this book. If you decide to focus on the hindered behaviour rather than on the underlying feelings, you have chosen to adopt the BMod approach and concentrate exclusively on the external conditions surrounding your behaviour. Indirectly, this could contribute to the modification of the feelings hindering the behaviour since it is likely that behaviour influences feelings as often as the other way round.

2. The option of suppressing unproductive feelings so that they do not hinder behaviour is not recommended. Suppression unnecessarily increases stress and does nothing to control or modify the underlying feelings. The reason why suppression is such a widespread practice is because most people do not know about the other alternatives; if you assume that there is little you can do to control your feelings, then there is really no viable alternative but to suppress the more unacceptable ones. The options we are going to explore in the remaining pages of this chapter are designed to prevent unproductive feelings. Suppression, therefore, becomes redundant.

3. Using relaxation techniques to release suppressed unproductive feelings

harmlessly is highly recommended, but it is an optional extra to the basic business of modifying feelings and behaviour. Also, the sheer number of alternative relaxation techniques makes it a subject for a book in its own right. If you want to find out more, I suggest you start by reading *The Relaxation Response*, a paperback by Dr Herbert Benson published by Fountain Books. In it he describes a straightforward relaxation technique that you could practise on your own if you wished.

Having dispensed with three out of the six options, I will concentrate for the rest of the chapter on showing you how to use the three that remain; they form the basis of FMod, which extends and complements the basic BMod approach.

Figure 10.3 illustrates the BMod model.

Figure 10.3

Figure 10.4 illustrates the FMod model.

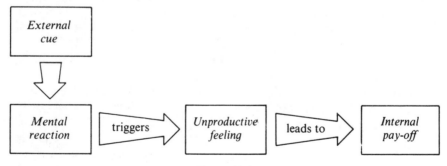

Figure 10.4

A combination of BMod and FMod gives the six boxes illustrated in Figure 10.1.

In the last chapter I introduced a step-by-step routine for using BMod; Table 10.1 provides a routine for using FMod on ourselves. Remember that you can use the FMod routine only on yourself as you do not have access to anyone else's feelings. BMod is for modifying other people's behaviour and your own behaviour; FMod is for the modification of only your own unproductive feelings.

THE FMOD ROUTINE FOR IDENTIFYING AND MODIFYING FEELINGS
THAT HINDER BEHAVIOUR

Table 10.1

FMod routine	Notes
1. Identify an unproductive feeling that hinders you often enough to be troublesome.	Start by centring attention on your behaviour. What aspects of your behaviour are you disappointed with? When do you know you could function at a more effective level? Then see if you can pin-point the feeling that is associated with the disappointing behaviour. This is often difficult because, in our language, we have fewer words to describe feelings than we have to describe actions. It does not matter if the description of the feeling is approximate; it is more important that you are certain the feeling hinders your performance and is, therefore, by definition, an unproductive one.
2. Identify what external cues trigger the unproductive feeling/ behaviour.	Answer the questions: 'When do I behave/feel like this?' and 'What situations or circumstances seem to trigger it?' Write down all the cues you can think of.
3. Identify the thoughts that come into your mind immediately prior to the onset of the feeling.	Work out what you think when you are exposed to the situations and circumstances identified in Step 2. The best way to do this is to slow down the thought process by trying to work out your inner dialogue. Do this by answering the question: 'If my thoughts were out loud, what sort of things would I hear myself saying in this situation prior to the onset of the unproductive feeling?'
4. Identify what pay-offs you tend to get after the hindered behaviour and the unproductive feeling.	Do this in two bites. First identify what happens after your hindered behaviour that is a satisfactory pay-off for you. Then identify what effect this has on your unproductive feeling. Usually, you will find that it is replaced with a more neutral or productive feeling.
5. Explore the possibility of avoiding, or minimizing your exposure to, the cues.	Go back to the cues you identified in Step 2. See if it is possible for you to avoid the cue situations altogether; if not, then see if you can at least minimize your exposure to them. Can you alter the cues so that they are less likely to trigger the unproductive feeling?
6. Explore the possibility of replacing the thoughts identified in Step 3 with new thoughts.	Go back to the 'inner dialogue' you spelt out in Step 3 and see if you can alter it so that it is less likely to trigger the unproductive feeling and more likely to trigger a neutral feeling. It is important not to expect too much here; the new thought should be aimed at neutralizing the unproductive feeling, not at reversing it 180° to something productive. So, if the unproductive feeling is one of misery, you should not expect to reverse it to one of ecstasy—your new thought should be designed to trigger a neutral feeling, neither miserable nor ecstatic.

127

Table 10.1 *continued*

FMod routine	*Notes*
7. Explore the possibility of changing the pay-offs that you experience after the hindered behaviour.	Go back to the pay-offs you identified in Step 4 and see if you can think of ways of changing both the external and internal pay-offs so that they are less likely to encourage repetition of both the unproductive feeling and the hindered behaviour. A useful question to answer is: 'What can I do to rearrange things so that I do not enjoy a pay-off after experiencing the unproductive feeling and/or after indulging in the hindered behaviour?' This is the most difficult part of the routine, and you might need help from a third party. For example, you might want someone deliberately to ignore you when your behaviour is under the influence of an unproductive feeling and thus deprive you of your attention-seeking pay-off.

SOME EXAMPLES OF THE FMOD ROUTINE IN PRACTICE

Let us start by returning to the example I gave earlier where the specialist was inhibited in putting forward a novel idea by unproductive feelings of anxiety. Referring to pages 121–122, you already have data for Steps 1, 2, 3 and 4 of the FMod routine. These steps encourage you to do a thorough analysis of the existing situation. Steps 5, 6 and 7 in the routine attempt to solve the problem. The specialist successfully modified his unproductive feeling as follows:

5. Avoiding/minimizing the cues. The specialist could not altogether avoid meetings where he was expected to act in an expert capacity; this was an integral part of his job. He did, however, modify the cue slightly but helpfully by arranging for the agenda items that involved him to be scheduled either at the beginning or at the end of the meeting. If they were at the beginning, this saved him from having to sit through earlier agenda items with anxiety building up. If they were at the end, he arranged to attend the meeting at the time that the agenda item in question was estimated to be under discussion. This was not as satisfactory, but it significantly reduced the time during which anxiety could be building up.

6. Exploring the possibility of replacing the thoughts that trigger the unproductive feeling. The earlier inner dialogue was: 'They all look as if they know what they are talking about. They are more senior, more experienced, more capable than I. I wonder if my idea is good enough? They will probably tear it to shreds. They are bound to make mincemeat of me. . . .'

The specialist examined this carefully and made two significant discoveries: there were thoughts anticipating the reaction to the *idea* and there were thoughts anticipating the reaction to *him*. It became clear that the thoughts anticipating adverse reactions to *him* were the ones triggering the feeling of anxiety. In this instance, these were: 'They are ... more capable than *I*' and 'They are bound to make mincemeat of *me*. . . .' Once he realized this, he decided to replace the old thoughts with new ones along the following lines: 'They all look as if they know what they are talking about. They are more senior and experienced than I— but not necessarily more capable. I wonder if they will take to my idea? I know it's a good idea, irrespective of whether they like it or not.'

This triggered a feeling of nil anxiety. The specialist, therefore, put forward his idea convincingly and enthusiastically.

7. Changing the pay-offs experienced after the behaviour. After the specialist had put forward his idea convincingly and enthusiastically, it was actively considered by the senior managers. In the event, they finished up rejecting the idea, but only after carefully weighing up all the pros and cons. This reaction was entirely acceptable to the specialist; the fact that his idea had been noticed, considered and then rejected was his pay-off, reinforcing the behaviour of putting forward ideas convincingly and enthusiastically.

Suppose, though, the worst had happened and, despite putting the idea forward strongly, the senior managers had still reacted by ignoring it. Our specialist could then change the internal pay-off by saying to himself something along the lines of: 'Oh well, you can't win them all I suppose! Let's see what I can learn from this. Did I present the idea in the best way? Could I have included more examples to illustrate its merits? Did I over-sell the idea? . . .'

Notice that the pay-off is to learn from the experience rather than to conduct a morbid self-denunciation. The absence of the unproductive feeling makes it less likely that the specialist will pillory himself and doubt his self-worth.

Figure 10.5 summarizes this case by putting BMod and FMod together in a six-box format.

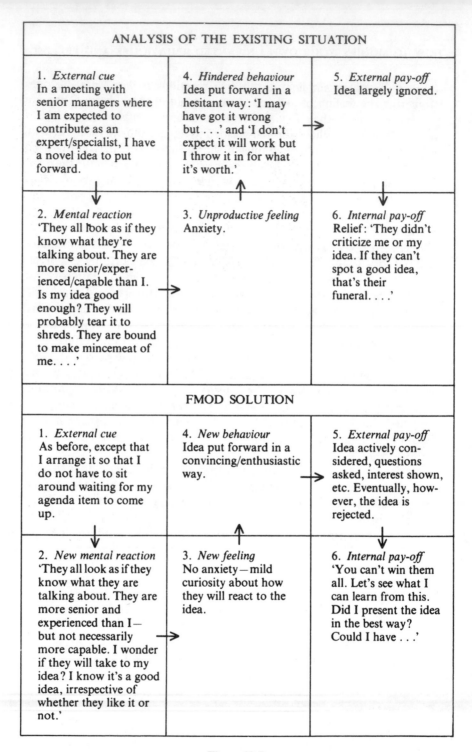

ANALYSIS OF THE EXISTING SITUATION		
1. *External cue* In a meeting with senior managers where I am expected to contribute as an expert/specialist, I have a novel idea to put forward.	4. *Hindered behaviour* Idea put forward in a hesitant way: 'I may have got it wrong but . . .' and 'I don't expect it will work but I throw it in for what it's worth.'	5. *External pay-off* Idea largely ignored.
2. *Mental reaction* 'They all look as if they know what they're talking about. They are more senior/exper-ienced/capable than I. Is my idea good enough? They will probably tear it to shreds. They are bound to make mincemeat of me. . . .'	3. *Unproductive feeling* Anxiety.	6. *Internal pay-off* Relief: 'They didn't criticize me or my idea. If they can't spot a good idea, that's their funeral. . . .'

FMOD SOLUTION		
1. *External cue* As before, except that I arrange it so that I do not have to sit around waiting for my agenda item to come up.	4. *New behaviour* Idea put forward in a convincing/enthusiastic way.	5. *External pay-off* Idea actively con-sidered, questions asked, interest shown, etc. Eventually, how-ever, the idea is rejected.
2. *New mental reaction* 'They all look as if they know what they are talking about. They are more senior and experienced than I — but not necessarily more capable. I wonder if they will take to my idea? I know it's a good idea, irrespective of whether they like it or not.'	3. *New feeling* No anxiety — mild curiosity about how they will react to the idea.	6. *Internal pay-off* 'You can't win them all. Let's see what I can learn from this. Did I present the idea in the best way? Could I have . . .'

Figure 10.5

If you find that this and other examples that follow do not ring true *for you*, then merely use them to check that you understand the FMod routine and get cracking as fast as you can on some of your own unproductive feelings. Since feelings are such personal, inner experiences, it is not at all surprising that the analysis of other people's feelings will strike you as tediously anecdotal. This is worth remembering, incidentally, when you are tempted to tell other people about your successes at modifying unproductive feelings! Naturally, you are interested in your own feelings, but remember that other people are primarily interested in their feelings—not yours.

Conscious that any examples I give are *other people's feelings* as far as you are concerned, Figures 10.6, 10.7 and 10.8 provide three further examples to illustrate how the FMod extension to BMod works.

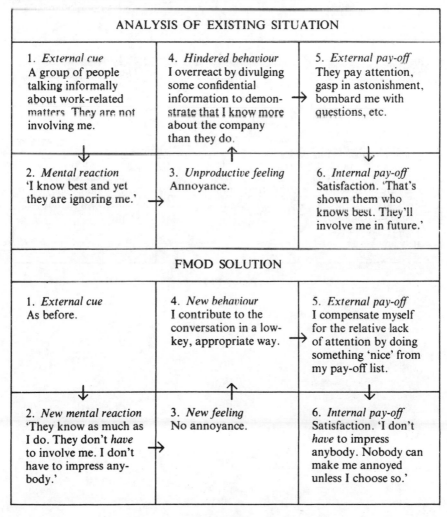

ANALYSIS OF EXISTING SITUATION		
1. *External cue* A group of people talking informally about work-related matters. They are not involving me.	4. *Hindered behaviour* I overreact by divulging some confidential information to demonstrate that I know more about the company than they do.	5. *External pay-off* They pay attention, gasp in astonishment, bombard me with questions, etc.
2. *Mental reaction* 'I know best and yet they are ignoring me.'	3. *Unproductive feeling* Annoyance.	6. *Internal pay-off* Satisfaction. 'That's shown them who knows best. They'll involve me in future.'
FMOD SOLUTION		
1. *External cue* As before.	4. *New behaviour* I contribute to the conversation in a low-key, appropriate way.	5. *External pay-off* I compensate myself for the relative lack of attention by doing something 'nice' from my pay-off list.
2. *New mental reaction* 'They know as much as I do. They don't *have* to involve me. I don't have to impress anybody.'	3. *New feeling* No annoyance.	6. *Internal pay-off* Satisfaction. 'I don't *have* to impress anybody. Nobody can make me annoyed unless I choose so.'

Figure 10.6

131

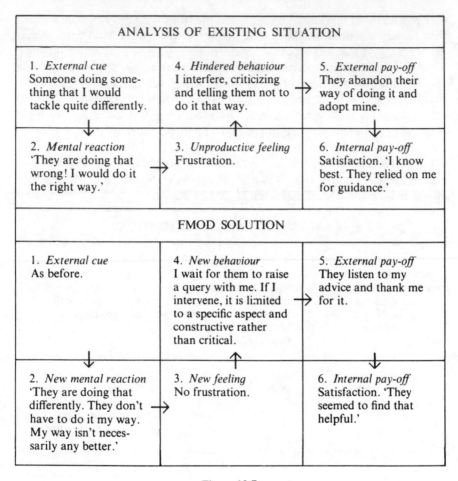

Figure 10.7

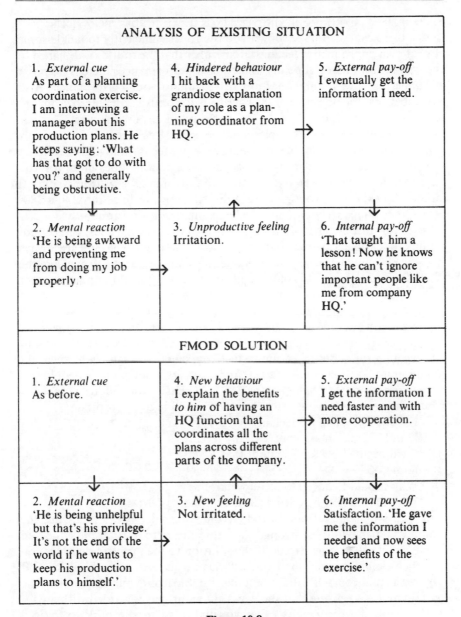

ANALYSIS OF EXISTING SITUATION		
1. *External cue* As part of a planning coordination exercise. I am interviewing a manager about his production plans. He keeps saying: 'What has that got to do with you?' and generally being obstructive.	4. *Hindered behaviour* I hit back with a grandiose explanation of my role as a planning coordinator from HQ.	5. *External pay-off* I eventually get the information I need.
2. *Mental reaction* 'He is being awkward and preventing me from doing my job properly.'	3. *Unproductive feeling* Irritation.	6. *Internal pay-off* 'That taught him a lesson! Now he knows that he can't ignore important people like me from company HQ.'
FMOD SOLUTION		
1. *External cue* As before.	4. *New behaviour* I explain the benefits *to him* of having an HQ function that coordinates all the plans across different parts of the company.	5. *External pay-off* I get the information I need faster and with more cooperation.
2. *Mental reaction* 'He is being unhelpful but that's his privilege. It's not the end of the world if he wants to keep his production plans to himself.'	3. *New feeling* Not irritated.	6. *Internal pay-off* Satisfaction. 'He gave me the information I needed and now sees the benefits of the exercise.'

Figure 10.8

133

FINAL POINTS ABOUT MODIFYING FEELINGS THAT HINDER BEHAVIOUR

I hope these examples have shown you the ropes sufficiently to tackle some of your own unproductive feelings. Remember that the routine is designed to alleviate feelings that frequently hinder your performance; there is no point in tampering with feelings that already facilitate your performance. Also remember that the objective of the routine is to control or 'neutralize' an unproductive feeling rather than to convert it into a productive one. This has been apparent in all the examples we have seen. Realistically, we can only hope to remove the hindrance of an unproductive feeling and in consequence behave more effectively; if, by any chance, the routine does more for you than this, it would be safer to regard the outcome as a welcome spin-off rather than expect the routine to turn unproductive feelings through a 180° turn. Other points to bear in mind when using the FMod routine are:

- Do not be disheartened if, having identified the external cues, you cannot think of feasible ways to avoid your exposure to them. The cues are always worth checking because you can sometimes think of a way to alleviate the cue situation, even if it is only slight. If you cannot avoid or alter the cues at all, then all is not lost; it means only that the mental reaction and pay-off aspects assume an even greater importance in your FMod solution.

- There is always mileage in identifying what mental reaction triggers the unproductive feeling. Replacing the mental reaction is often the key to preventing the onset of an unproductive feeling. Always try to spell out the mental reaction *in full* as a verbatim passage of inner dialogue. No one can write your inner dialogues for you—you have to do that for yourself— but here are some useful catchphrases to build in as appropriate:

   'No one can *make* me feel anything.'
   'I, and I alone, am in charge of my feelings.'
   'I will decide how to feel about that.'
   'I am OK.'
   'Why should I choose to feel upset?'
   'Why should I let *him* decide how I am going to feel?'

- As you will realize from BMod, if the external pay-off following the hindered behaviour is strong, the temptation to repeat the hindered behaviour will also be strong. If the solution to the problem deprives you of the original pay-off, then you will have to insert an 'artificial' pay-off by rewarding yourself with something suitable from your pay-off list. The vital thing is to ensure that the new behaviour gets rewarded with a pay-off; if not, the prediction is that you will tend to slip back to the old (hindered) way of behaving.

Let me finish with a couple of general points to put FMod in its proper perspective. Remember that FMod is for your own personal use; you cannot use the FMod approach to modify someone else's feelings because you only have access to the external events and that limits you to BMod. Certainly

encourage other people to modify their unproductive feelings—but they must do it, not you. Here is a summary of when to use BMod and FMod:
- When other people's behaviour is giving you a problem—use BMod.
- When your own behaviour is giving you a problem—use BMod.
- When your own feelings are giving you a problem—use FMod.

As you have seen, this book is mainly about how to use the BMod approach to solve the problems you have with other people. In this final chapter, we have looked fleetingly at applying BMod and FMod to yourself. If you would like to read other books on the last two in particular, I recommend the following:
- For BMod on yourself: *The Success Factor* by Dr Robert Sharpe and David Lewis, published by Pan in paperback.
- For FMod: *A New Guide to Rational Living* by Dr Albert Ellis and Dr Robert Harper, published by the Wilshire Book Company in paperback.

Modifying your own behaviour and feelings is an uphill struggle, but surely it is worth it?

Index

Aggressive behaviour, 3–4, 33–40
Annoyance, 131
Anxiety, 122, 128–129, 130
Appraisal, 9, 62, 65–69
Attitudes, 12–15, 18–19, 34, 89
Autocratic behaviour, 3–4, 33–40

Bad timekeeping, 75
Behaviour:
  causes of, 88–91
  definition of, 17–19
  explanations of, 12–16
  influence of the environment on, 53–57
Behaviour therapy, 75–76
Behaviour Modification (BMod):
  advantages of, 40–42
  aims of, 17
  basic principles of, 76–82
  ethics of, 93
  examples of, 25–28, 30–48, 100–112
  history of, 71–76
  limitations of, 85–88
  objections to, 88–97
  of yourself, 114–118
  routine for, 98–100
Behaviour shaping, 74–75
Beliefs, 34, 89
Blaming others, 105–106, 111

Circumvention, 2, 22, 27–28, 106–107, 112
Coaching, 9 (see also Appraisal)
Common sense, 96–97
Conditioning, 72–73
Consequences (see Pay-offs)
Contingency concept, 61–62, 76–77, 82
Counselling, 9 (see also Appraisal)
Courses 9–10
Creativity, lack of, 50–52
Criticism, 106–107
Cues, definition of, 19–22

Deadlines, failure to meet, 5, 46–48
Decentralization, 64
Defensive behaviour, 105–106, 111
Delegation, 55–56

Elusiveness, 101–102, 108
Extinction, 73, 78

Feelings:
  and behaviour, 12–15, 18–19, 89–91, 118
  assumptions about, 119–120

facts about, 120–121
pay-offs for, 124
suppression of, 119, 123
Feelings modification:
  examples of, 130–133
  of yourself, 117–135
  routine for, 127–128
Frustration, 132

Graduates, induction of, 50–51

Hesitancy, 121–122, 128–129, 130

Irritation, 133

Learning, 23, 89, 121

Management practices, 58–70
Manipulation, 91–93
Meetings, 53–55
Money, 61
Motives, 12–15, 18–19, 89
Motivation, 61, 62–63

Nagging others, 2, 21, 25–27
Needs, 14–15, 62–63
Negative behaviour, 19–20, 23–25

Objective setting, 55–56
Overdependence, 102–103, 109
Overloading people, 4–5, 42–45

Pay-offs:
  explanation of, 23–28
  long term v. short term, 60–62
  (see also Reinforcement; Rewards)
Pavlov, Ivan, 72–73
People, management of, 58–70
People-problems:
  creation of, 50–57
  criteria for, 7
  definition of, 1–2
  pinpointing of, 11–12
  (see also Problems)
Pep-talks, 8–9
Performance, 13–15, 62–63 (see also Behaviour and Problems)
Personality, 11–13, 18
Personnel administration, 63
Planning, 55–56
Precedents, 63
Procrastination, 79–80, 100–101, 107, 117

136

Problems:
  aggressive behaviour, 3–4, 33–40
  annoyance, 131
  anxiety, 122, 128–129, 130
  autocratic behaviour, 3–4, 33–40
  bad timekeeping, 75
  blaming others, 105–106, 111
  circumvention, 2, 22, 27–28, 106–107, 112
  creativity, lack of, 50–52
  criticism, 106–107
  deadlines, 5, 46–48
  defensive behaviour, 105–106, 111
  delegation, 55–56
  elusiveness, 101–102, 108
  frustration, 132
  hesitancy, 121–122, 128–129, 130
  irritation, 133
  meetings, 53–55
  nagging others, 2, 21, 25–27
  negative behaviour, 19–20, 23–25
  overdependence, 102–103, 109
  overloading people, 4–5, 42–45
  planning, 55–56
  procrastination, 79–80, 100–101, 107, 117
  reluctance,
    to make decisions, 102–103, 109
    to manage, 55–56
    to volunteer, 52–53
  reticence, 103–104
  secretiveness, 106–107
  strikes, 61–62
  stroppy behaviour, 2, 21–22, 27
  verbose reports, 65–69
Problem solving, model for, 29
Punishment, 10, 59–60, 78–80

Redundancy, 10
Relaxation techniques, 123–124, 126

Reluctance:
  to make decisions, 102–103, 109
  to manage, 55–56
  to volunteer, 52–53
Reflex actions, 71
Reinforcement:
  combination strategies, 78–79
  continuous, 81–82
  experiments in, 73–75
  intermittent, 81–82
  positive and negative, 74, 77–78
  schedules of, 74 (*see also* Pay-offs)
Reticence, 103–104
Rewards, 50–57, 58–60
  (*see also* Pay-offs)

Salary administration, 61
Sanctions (*see* Punishment)
Sechenev, Ivan, 71
Secretiveness, 106–107
Self-control, 95
Skinner, B. F., 74, 76, 77
Stimulus Response theory (*see* Conditioning)
Strikes, 61–62
Stroppy behaviour, 2, 21–22, 27

Trade unions, 62
Training, 9–10
Thorndike, Edward, 73–74, 77
Time Management, 94–95

Volunteering, 52
Verbose reports, 65–69

Watson, John, 73

Yourself, modification of, 114–118